# THE MOTHER-IN-LAW DAUGHTER-IN-LAW CONFLICT

---

## The Exploration and Improvement of the Mother-In-Law—Daughter-In-Law Relationship

By

### Dr. Joseph Morris

This book is a work of non-fiction. Names and places have been changed to protect the privacy of all individuals. The events and situations are true.

ISBN: 1-4107-7952-1 (e-book)
ISBN: 1-4107-7951-3 (Paperback)

This book is printed on acid free paper.

1stBooks - rev. 11/13/03

# About the Author

Dr. Joseph Morris is a Family Counselor and Therapist. He has written four books, as well as professional articles. He has been Editor-in-Chief of a professional monthly magazine. He has had his humor published in many magazines.

He has been blessed with a close, loving family, a wonderful marriage, precious children, all married, and a large gaggle of delightful grandchildren.

# Table of Contents

# <u>Dedication</u>

This book is dedicated to mothers-in-law and daughters-in-law everywhere who are struggling for mutual warmth, closeness, and understanding.

This book is particularly dedicated to four wonderful human beings: my incredible sons-in-law and daughters-in-law.

# Introduction

There is excitement in the air. A young couple is in love. The wedding is exquisite. Two large families meet and have the celebration. The festivities go on and on. The future holds so much promise. The newlyweds set up their first home. The community welcomes their arrival. The relatives look for every opportunity to get together and bask in the newness of it all. There are parties. There are gifts. The holidays take on an extra special meaning, with the fledgling couple being the guests of honor, the focus of all the attention. Soon, if they are blessed, babies arrive on the scene, again a reason to cheer. More parties. More prayers of appreciation. The present and the future are alive. More additions to the combined happy families.

Somewhere, in the midst of all the pleasantries, oddly enough, there is a cloud present. In many families, like a common thread appearing again and again, there is a problem between two individuals. Sometimes the problem appears out in the open. Sometimes it lurks beneath, like the positive and negative poles on a magnet. Like oil and water, there are two family members who do not easily mix. They are the new bride and her mother-in-law. Their frequent antagonism is a well known but infrequently spoken about syndrome. Their clash with one another is classic. It is built-in. It is complicated. It is very real, and must be dealt with.

Put two young mothers together on a park bench watching their toddlers play. They will chat and share their goings on. In no time, they will get to the topic of their mothers-in-law. There will follow a rapid flow of grievances that they experience with these older women. They will laugh and cry sharing their misery. They will be amazed at how similar their feelings are. They will share horror stories that almost mirror one another. They will wonder why they never knew about this spoiler of a relationship beforehand. Why were they not forewarned? Oh sure, the comics they heard always included the usual mother-in-law jokes. However, these jokes always originated from the son-in-law's perspective. (Like the definition of a mixed feeling: Your mother-in-law going over a cliff driving your brand new car!) Never was heard a sneer from a daughter-in-law.

Similarly, just put two middle-aged women with married sons together and they will rapidly find a camaraderie they might never have had before. They cannot believe how disappointed they are with their new daughters-in-law. How could this have happened? They raised their sons with the best of their ability. How could their sons have selected so poorly? The women share. They counsel each other. They laugh. They cry. They are in pain.

In an otherwise happy world, the mother-in-law and daughter-in-law have an awful attitude toward one another. They are truly surprised. They had no preparation. Their reactions to one another are strong, and they find this having a terrible negative effect on their broad outlook about their joint family. They may be ashamed about their feelings, but the feelings will not go away. They find themselves in a real inner war, and there seems to be no easy solution in sight.

Yes, the mother-in-law—daughter-in-law conflict is real. It is common. It is very complicated. With every two different individuals with different makeup come very different ramifications. How deep the wounds and subsequent scars are experienced varies greatly. This book attempts to analyze the many aspects of this conflict. The chapters review many of the variables—history, parents, baggage, siblings and other surrounding influences.

The intention of the author is to present the multiple issues in a logical, objective and analytic fashion. The analysis intends to lay out all the factors from the vantage point of both combatants, and allows the reader to make his or her own evaluation and judgment.

However, somewhere in the investigative process, certain truisms appeared. The book seemed to stray from an original neutral stance into a certain direction. The author found the facts pulling from the starting, non-judgmental state, and leading to definite conclusions. In addition, the gloom about the entire subject began to lift, and justifiably so. This is indeed wonderful for everyone concerned.

The book ends with a sampling of actual live interviews with mothers-in-law and daughters-in-law. The interviews are unedited and unabridged.

## The Engagement is Announced

The announcement of their engagement was both expected and a shock. Everyone knew it was coming, but the official new status was a major, dramatic development. The prince was conquered. The catch of the century was now taken. No longer would he be the subject of parents of eligible daughters who whispered regularly behind his back. The top name on the list of most matchmakers was sadly erased by these entrepreneurs. What a happy moment, except for the young lasses who kept up hope that this dreamy bachelor might notice them.

The future bride's parents were overjoyed. They had worried for years that everyone else's children in their community were getting married at such young ages except their own. Why had they not been blessed? Until this point, none of their children was even close to having a serious relationship. Finally, finally they could relax. Their daughter, a future daughter-in-law, was finally settled.

Their extended family was in a state of celebration. They could barely contain themselves with all the excitement. Yes, their daughter and they themselves were normal after all.

What of the parents of the prince, the future groom? They had the discomfort of very mixed feelings. Of course, they publicly cheered. After all, their son would not be one of those young men who never got married but rather found comfort in the packed crowd of singles that seemed to hang around forever. He would settle down, have a wife to care for him and to stand behind him in these difficult formative years. He could stop his exhausting dating which he had no strength for anymore, but seemed to continue only at their pleading. He could relax, focus, and have stability, finally, finally after years of search. He could bring them much joy by heading a new family and fathering grandchildren who would carry on their family name.

But...his selection of a girl to marry shocked them out of their shoes. She seemed sweet and honest and obviously adored their son. (Then again, everyone who had met their son adored him.) She was reasonably attractive and came from a decent family. They suffered with great pain over and over to get an answer to the question they obsessed over. Was this the best he could do? This was the object of his long quest?

Their son was the object of admiration of the immediate world (and farther) and this woman was his final selection?? In truth, they had expected a princess, at least a Grace Kelly. They expected a girl who exuded radiance and charm and majesty. Why had he rushed, they wondered (though they conceded that he seemed to be dating

6

forever). Why didn't he date her longer to get to know her better to really be sure (although six months was admittedly, much longer than a lot of kids dated before they tied the knot). Maybe he was just too physically tired to think clearly when it came to a selection, given his long work hours and his long trip to her house. Maybe he had his fill of dating at some point, and he succumbed to the first half-normal girl that came along.

Our future mother-in-law took this engagement very hard. She longed to undo it, but she was trapped. Anything negative that she said or did would inflict great pain on her son. Likewise, it would stir a sleeping lion in her husband who sometimes overdid his support of her when she was unhappy. For sure, any visible hostility would be picked up instantly by her future daughter-in-law. This might prove fatal in terms of long term close relationships between the future families.

The future groom's mother goes into a great depression. Privately, of course. It seemed like a lifetime of dreams had been cast aside in one fell swoop. She had tried so hard to be a good person. She prided herself in being a role model that would make her children and friends proud of her. What lay ahead for her were the frequent get-togethers of the families of the bride and groom, to bask in the joy of the joining of their two worlds. What also was coming up were the endless sessions between daughter-in-law and mother-in-law in the selection of wedding preparations—clothing for members of the wedding party, the catering hall, the ushers and bridesmaids, the menu, and the seating. She felt that she didn't have the strength to go

7

through with it with any kind of pleasantness. She felt weak, betrayed, alone.

Publicly, she was forever the lady. She beamed to her friends. She crowed to her relatives. She chatted with them all about the new family she would soon be connected to. She discussed some of the decisions as they were being made regarding the forthcoming ceremony.

# The Mother-In-Law's Expectations

The mother-in-law enters the relationship with her daughter-in-law with some spoken or, more usually, unspoken expectations. Broadly, she expects the new addition to follow the pattern of her other children and in-law children. In the busy, anxious weeks before the wedding, the mother-in-law is overwhelmed with the emotional impact of her son getting married and setting up his own home. She is likewise pre-occupied with the wedding plans—meetings with her future daughter-in-law's parents, the caterer, the florist and the dressmaker. The actual future relationship with her daughter-in-law has no time priority and therefore is not focused on amidst the other goings on. (In truth, it does come up frequently in some cases where the mother-in-law and daughter-in-law work together before the marriage in the areas of selecting and furnishing the future dwelling of the couple, picking out flower arrangements, selection of gown colors, etc.)

Let us set up a hypothetical family of two parents and three children, girl, boy and girl. The mother, a future mother-in-law, is at the center of the bringing up of the children and running the home. We will assume that the mother and father love each other and have worked out (does it ever end?) their own relationship. This has taken the usual enormous effort that is necessary for two young people, each with a heavy load of pre-marital baggage, to make so as to fulfill the needs of the other. Like most fathers, <u>our</u> father here, the future father-in-law, is mostly just not around. He is at work, at the gym, or squirreled away in some nook working on his computer. He is a good man and does the right things. In the average family, he is a lesser factor in the bringing up of his children because of his unavailability, and more so, his usually more modest skills of communication and sensitivity. The mother goes through the usual steps of clothing and feeding her kids, and dealing with their problems, their homework and their health needs. Besides all that, she works very hard at instilling in them what she considers proper values. She wants them to be fine human beings. She adjusts their thinking and mindsets in many different areas, pushing, always pushing, in the direction that she deems will bring them to their highest potential. This includes the areas of friendships, respect for others and developing fine character. She also attempts to be a role model as a grown woman, to do the right things and say the right things. Often, all this is done while juggling her own job and trying to keep the house in good shape. In her home, she attempts to create neatness, orderliness, and a predictable routine, with the cooperation of all the family members.

She is the usual leader in the family shopping, whether it be food, everyone's clothing, furniture or general supplies. She develops the responsibility for making the home run smoothly at the same time that she is developing herself as a person, a wife, a mother, an employee and a member of her community.

She raises her children to follow the pattern that she has set up, allowing, of course, for their own individuality, limitations, and talents. She has a general expectation that when her daughters get married, they will conduct their lives in the same general framework that she has conducted her own. Our mother anticipates that her daughters will train their future husbands and children properly as she did (!). She expects that when she walks into the kitchen of one of her married daughters one day, the style of cooking, layout of dishes and pots, utensils, recipes, color scheme and appliances of her child would be a similar, though granted up-dated, version of her own. The meals they serve would probably be in the same overall selection of flavors and ingredients as the home they grew up in.

Clothing the children, dealing with laundry and cleaning, and maintaining the physical aspects of the home would probably be a continuation of the family pattern, she assumes. The scheduling of recreation, religious observances, frequency of guests in the home, which developed into a comfortable pattern over a period of time, would probably continue.

Our mother, the future mother-in-law, predicts with some certainty that her married daughters would communicate to the husbands that, in a broad sense, this is how they want to run their homes. Her two future sons-in-law, she calculates, like most husbands, have their priorities elsewhere, and would be happy to have their new wives make the decisions on domestic issues. Even though the sons-in-law come from environments that their mothers had set up in their homes, which are very different, they usually, sooner or later, with or without much struggle, would give in to their wives' preferences, and justifiably so, after all. As we said earlier, it is the mother of the house who is the domestic general, while the father is the capable foreign minister.

As for her son, her only son in our hypothetical choice of family, she would anticipate that his living style, likewise, would fit into the familiar pattern. Her son, who loves her cooking, would probably expect and therefore request from his new wife to repeat the familiar. If he is used to repeated variations of meat and vegetables, so it shall be. If he has grown up on salads and pasta, he will request these selections from his future wife. If he had a steady diet of Mediterranean-spiced food, he will teach his new bride, our future daughter-in-law, that the heart of a man is in his stomach, and so his preference must prevail.

The son, likewise, would set the tone in their daily living style, we expect. If he is used to a week filled with sports, movies and family hikes, this would repeat. If he is comfortable with daily family dinners at a predictable time, spiced with lively family discussions and debate, he will push for its continuation. If he is spoiled by having had his dresser contents neatly folded by his mother on a regular basis, including socks and underwear, he will expect this service in his home.

In effect, the mother is setting up a double standard. Her theme is the continuation of her family's pattern. In a way, she is inconsistent at the same time that she is relentless. For the purpose of perpetuity, she expects her daughters to be the leaders in the repeat of her teachings as far as their families are concerned. After all, the women run the home. However, when it comes to her son, the rules change. Now the <u>husband</u> must be the dominant domestic partner. It is her son's preferences, values, style of living and principles, all of which came from her, that must prevail.

Therein lies the basis of a massive problem. The individuality of her daughter-in-law is not in the new mother-in-law's reckoning. Conveniently or unconsciously, it is overlooked or dismissed as not having any merit. Our hypothetical mother-in-law anticipates walking into her son's future home and witnessing the same scenario as she sees in her daughters' homes. It is a rude awakening for the mother-in-law. It is crushing, infuriating and instantly unacceptable to the mother-in-law to see any variant.

# The Daughter-In-Law's Expectations

Our hypothetical daughter-in-law is in her low 20s. She has grown up presumably with siblings. In the majority of cases, her parents are married, both working and nearing age fifty. She has possibly gone to college, depending on the family's financial situation, and possibly has post-graduate education or training.

She has recently met the love of her life. He is a little older and taller than she. He is a handsome hunk of a guy. He has, unbelievably, most everything she ever wanted in a man. He is hard working, honest, likes children, has a sense of humor, has a sense of purpose, and is religious. Best of all, by far, is the fact that he totally adores her. He thinks she is the most gorgeous female on earth. He cannot take his eyes off her and when he is away from her, he calls her what seems to be every five minutes.

After a brief courtship, she shamelessly proposed to him. She calculated that (a) like a typical young man his age, he needed a little prodding to make a commitment; (b) she did not want to risk losing him to some prettier hussy that came along. They were engaged all winter and agreed that a June wedding would best fit into their work and school projected schedules.

The future bride had a good relationship with her parents and most of the time with her siblings. Being relatively ambitious, she seemed to spend less and less time at home. When home, she spent much time helping her mother who was saddled with bringing up her younger siblings, keeping the house running, and managing a job. Her father was a good man whom she looked up to. He was a little bit hard to relate to and seemed to be off in his own world most of the time. She was very comfortable with the tone that her mother set up in the house. She liked the way the house was furnished and the meals that her mother prepared. She admired her mother's tireless ability to juggle work and home needs. She liked her honesty, straightforwardness, and her ability to show affection. She agreed with most of the values that mom stood for and generally, looked back at her upbringing as being a decent, content experience.

She did disagree with her mother in many areas. She didn't feel that she focused hard enough on her kids' feelings or at least give them enough time to elicit these feelings. She seemed to lack style in the choice of colors and patterns in the decor of the rooms. Her cooking, while wholesome, was by far too laden with saturated fats. She was totally ignorant, incredibly, when it came to using a computer for even the most mundane tasks. However, all in all, she could count on her mother as a helpful friend whenever she needed her, and at this time of her life, she really needed her.

Mom spent several consecutive weekends exploring wedding hall choices. Ever so patiently, her mom went with her as she tried out different bridal gown shops until they finally agreed on a suitable gown. They sat together at the printer selecting invitations, print style, and wording. They even chatted about marriage itself. Mom shared some of her highlights and some of her sadnesses. As if to prepare her for the future, mom even confided with her about some disappointed aspects of life with her dad, well as some dreams that would never be fulfilled. For the first time in a long while, they had some really close sharing conversations.

Our future daughter-in-law met her future in laws at a mini-celebration of her fiance's birthday, a Broadway show followed by dessert at a nearby restaurant. Conceptually, this was the beginning of an awesome expansion of her world. She was adding not only her lifetime partner, but his parents, his two sisters, his uncles, aunts and cousins and all the connected in-law relatives. What had she pictured his parents and siblings would be like? How would she relate? How would she feel with now having <u>four</u> parents? How would she get along with her future sisters-in-law? After all, they would be closest to her own age. She couldn't wait to have her own children. How would they impact on all these relationships?

Her family had problems with some of their relatives. At any family gatherings or with even mention of these individuals' names, bad vibes immediately were felt. There was bad talk and occasional confrontations, all of which always made her want to disappear some place. She could not handle fighting and she vowed to fill her life with only friendly people around her. She would be the family's peacemaker in the future.

Her future mother-in-law? As of the day she announced her engagement, she had never yet met this woman. What did she picture about her mother-in-law or any mother-in-law? Frankly, she hadn't given it much thought. A mother-in-law was just part of a big package of people that were connected to her future husband. A mother-in-law never got any more forethought than a father-in-law or brother-in-law. She was in the big group. After all, her future mother-in-law was not an additional mother. She had one already, and she was close with her. Would she ever have a problem here? Absolutely not.

First of all, our future bride considered herself someone who could get along with almost anybody. Second, she modestly admitted to herself that almost everyone loved her—instantly. She was that kind of a person. Third, if this woman conceived and bore her son, the fiancé, that credential alone, though merely biological, made her, theoretically at least, the best woman in the world next to her own mother. Fourth, even though she had a mind of her own, she felt that anyone her husband liked, she would automatically like. What was his was hers. Her guy was so fantastic that she would be honored to be part of whatever he was connected to. Fifth, a mother-in-law relationship didn't feel like a particularly important one. After all, she, the daughter-in-law, would be setting up an independent home with her husband in a location the two select, and raising her future children in the manner that they, the future parents, felt was of the highest quality. Her future mother-in-law would be distracted and immersed in her own adult world. It was true that the future daughter-in-law did have married friends that shared different degrees of problems with their respective mothers-in-law. It was true that some of the stories she heard were really awful. However, all this had little impact on her. She wasn't <u>there</u> yet. She was still a single girl with a relatively uncomplicated, uncluttered life. Connection on any meaningful level seemed far away, if at all. Sixth, as mentioned before, if she were going to be connected to any members of this new family that had any kind of emotional impact on her, it would be rather with her sisters-in-law. They were her generation. Their kids would grow up together. They would help each other. There might be some rivalry or jealousy that might intrude, but they would be only of the minor, normal magnitude. By far more important and immediate would be the interaction of her, the daughter-in-law's siblings and their mates with her husband's siblings and their husbands and wives.

Seventh, if she gave the subject of her future daughter-in-law - mother-in-law relationship an occasional serious thought, her future mother-in-law, she pictured, would be an extension of her mother, though one step removed. She would be caring, tolerant, generous, encouraging, interested, complimentary, supportive, protective, helpful, understanding, friendly, responsible, forgiving, clear thinking, stimulating, loving, affectionate, fun, pleasant, approachable, available, aware, happy, sincere, modest, cheerful, flexible, resourceful, enterprising, honest, thoughtful, considerate, imaginative, sensitive, organized, relaxed, energetic, calm, compassionate, and eternally grateful that she was graced with such a daughter-in-law.

Meanwhile back at the birthday celebration evening of theatre and good food and meeting her future father-in-law and mother-in-law for the first time, all of the above crashed with a loud thud.

# The Boy in Between

The connecting link between mother-in-law and daughter-in-law is a young man in his early twenties. He is "THE SON". He has grown up in a reasonably normal family. He has an older and younger sister. The older sister, like many a first born, is in her own world. She focuses <u>out</u> of the family, to friends, school, activities and where she is heading in life. She does not look back at her younger brother and sister. She loves them, but they are too young and too attached yet to their parents to play any significant role in her life at this time.

His younger sister likewise does not have a major impact on his life. First of all, she is a girl. Her second offense is that she is a teenager. Her daily concerns—boys, her hair, pimples, fashion, clothes, good friends, difficult friends, so-so friends, and homework—all seem like a different world, even though they grew up together in the same house. His sisters, though not especially connected to him, love him very much. They focus on him and his interests, mostly when he is in trouble or unhappy or hurting over something or another.

Our young man is very much the focus of his parents. After all, he is the only boy. He alone will carry on the family name. They adore him. He is gentle, kind, still pure, and possesses what they feel sometimes is too much integrity. In the eyes of both the boy and his parents, his upbringing has been a happy one—traditional, with good focus, with lots of love. He has done well at college and has just completed graduate school. His mother and father watch his progress closely. While in the specific domestic areas, his sisters are closer to their Mom and Dad, he has a special role in his parents' eyes. He will some day head his own family, carrying on the tradition that he grew up with. He will be the torchbearer. He will represent the next generation as the product of his parents' training and guidance. He will always be the apple of their eyes. He will make them proud. His achievements will reflect the efforts and sacrifices of the doting parents that stand behind him.

What is in his head? The usual agenda of a young man. First and foremost, he has had the powerful need to do well in school and to establish himself in his new profession. That is the structure and badge of achievement that obsesses young males; and the degree of success in this area, determines to a great extent his self-esteem and self-confidence. He loves ball playing. He is naturally gifted in this area, although he is too modest to absorb it. With the increase of other more pressing commitments, he is always desperate to find playing time. He feels pressed to maintain his physical fitness, and when he can play, he is able to let off some steam and enjoy the competitiveness that is strongly built into him.

His career and athletics use up almost all of his time. As noted earlier, he spends some quality time with his sisters, but they are never usually around. His father and mother are great people in his eyes. They, too, are preoccupied with their adult world. He does, however, feel their strong love. He knows all too well that he is the "family prince". While enjoying this coveted position, he is often uncomfortable with the special scrutiny that his parents give him. He feels the pressure to be good, in fact, to be perfect, and to always produce the enormous accomplishments they seem constantly to expect of him. He has friends, but like most males, they are "activity" friends. They are individuals he studies with, he travels with, he plays ball with or he goes camping with. Unlike girls' experiences of friends, he does not share feelings or concerns or fears with them. Emotions are kept inside. In fact, he takes pride in not showing emotion, positive or negative, to those around him. That's a "girl thing", he perceives.

Hobbies and recreating for the most part are in the past or in the future. Time constraints put them on the back burner for now. They seem too frivolous for a young man rapidly transforming from childhood into adulthood.

Ta Da!! He has just met the love of his life, his first love, in fact. He has been bowled over like he has never experienced before. Sure, he has dated occasionally when time permitted or when his parents insisted, but this is it! He met a young lady at a wedding who happened to be seated next to his older sister. When he went over to his sister at the end of the ceremony, he was introduced. He looked into her eyes and heard her voice, and he was instantly overwhelmed. She was so dazzling that he could not look at her. When he said something, he involuntarily went into a stutter. He was paralyzed and very smitten, and instantly, the wedding he was attending, the bride and groom, his relatives and the hundreds of guests all seemed to disappear. This was his first experience of such virtual madness in his young life. After what seemed like an eternity, he re-entered the world of the wedding that night hoping he hadn't made too much of a fool of himself.

They dated for six months. She was taking post-graduate courses. He was working very long hours at his first post-graduate job. Their get-togethers always seemed like stolen moments, special because they were difficult to come by. Of course, the two were usually overtired, sacrificing sleep to fit in work and play. She lived some distance away, so they met at some location in between their homes. Usually, though, he traveled to her house to pick her up. She met his parents only a few times during their courtship, while he had many opportunities while at her home to spend time with her parents and siblings.

# Preparation for the Wedding

She spent quite a lot of time with her future daughter-in-law, even more so than with her son. The wedding event is, after all, really a woman's event down to the finest detail. (Any male involved merely has to rent a tuxedo that fits the day before the happy event, and he is totally taken care of and acceptable.) She found her daughter-in-law surprisingly immature when it came to decision making. On one hand, she had trouble making <u>any</u> decision. On the other hand, when she did make a decision, it always seemed like the wrong one. In her conversations with her daughter-in-law, she found herself staring at her a lot, trying to analyze those features that attracted her son to her.

What poor taste the girl seemed to have. Her sense of color was odd. She looked at flowers with seemingly such distance that it seemed that she never had walked through a flowery meadow during her lifetime. She was little help with the menu, bordering on being a vegetarian. She seemed to have very little sense of what people liked, much less thought. How could she participate in choices that would please the wedding guests if she has so little insight?

Then again, our suffering mother-in-law backed off a bit and tried to be objective. Was she fair? Was she too harsh on the inexperienced young lady? Was she expecting too much? How would this babe in the woods be expected to make any decision with so few life experiences? Was she, the older one, any better than she was at this age? Was she allowing for a difference of opinion, another perspective? Was she too intolerant of the desires of another individual? Could she see past her own firm convictions?

These bouts of fair objective introspection did not last too long. Her pain or really her anger took over all too quickly. These sessions with her daughter-in-law and sometime with her daughter-in-law's parents were too painful. She often felt that she didn't have the strength to continue. Yet, so much was at stake. The evening of the wedding of the prince had to be perfect. Her many friends and relatives would be there.

In making the many choices during the preparation stage, the mother-in-law continued to have a hard time. For example, at the printer, while she preferred an elegant understated lettering type, her partner in making these decisions and her mother pushed for a casual script style. Where she strongly admired the traditional line up of sentences which gave the reader exact information as to time and place of reception and ceremony, the others liked an informal layout which was not only child-like but omitted a few basic pieces of necessary information. She liked classic black on white. The others? Blue lining the envelopes. Blue? For a son's wedding? She was horrified. Her future in-laws likewise insisted on a folksy paragraph at the end to the invited guests which had some vague theme like "Peace on Earth". She could not talk them out of it. She was so embarrassed even thinking about the reactions her close friends and relatives would have when they opened the invitation.

She was surprised at her newfound intolerance. She always considered herself a very flexible person when it came to dealing with others. She was always anxious to please, to make the next one happy. So, invariably, she had always given in to others who had a strong opinion about something. With rare exception, she could live with the strong preferences of others if it made for peace and harmony. In the scenario of shopping and preparing with her future daughter-in-law and her family, her inner pain was so strong that her giving nature all but disappeared. Rather, she exhibited impatience, stubbornness, and argumentativeness. She was no longer "Mrs. Goody Two Shoes". She was now the type person she abhorred. She was a fighter. Giving in was out of the question. This was war. "My son," she wearily asked, "what have you done?"

# Visiting Her Son's Apartment Two Years after the Wedding

Visiting the apartment of her son and daughter-in-law was a periodic necessary gesture that she anticipated with great pain. Our mother-in-law had somehow survived the wedding day. She had survived the customary week of daily mini-banquets that followed. She had swallowed the young couple's selection of apartment and the block that they were to reside on. She had survived her daughter-in-law's style (or lack thereof) of decorating her apartment. She dealt with her daughter-in-law's pregnancy. (That's another long strange story.) She was overjoyed with the precious baby girl that arrived about a year ago. The latter celebration admittedly was tempered by two aspects. One was that the baby girl looked exactly like the daughter-in-law's mother. Second, the baby was named after the daughter-in-law's favorite prophetess in the bible rather one of a list of cherished deceased relatives waiting for a baby to be named after them.

Meanwhile back at the visit, the mother-in-law arrives, by appointment on a Sunday, with her husband, the father-in-law. The father-in-law did always enjoy visiting his married children, although at this destination, he knew that he was invited by his wife for desperately needed emotional support. One foot in the door he, of course, was immediately reminded of one of his favorite jokes which he always told his teenage daughter when he made the mistake of entering her bedroom and was faced with the incredible state of disarray. Showing excellent taste and restraint, he did not let this joke leave his lips lest he upset his son whom he adored.

The scene of the apartment, which evoked this favorite joke of his, was no exaggeration. The mother-in-law saw a living environment which was an exact opposite of what she orchestrated when a guest walked into <u>her</u> home. In the home of the mother-in-law, everything was neat in appearance. There was no clutter. The surfaces were dusted. Though not to a fanatical degree, she always wanted the look of cleanliness and orderliness. Not so, by far, was the scene she witnessed walking into this "training" apartment. It had the look of a dwelling designed by the prevailing star of the young family, the year old toddler. It was difficult to take two straight steps forward. There was so much on the floor. Teddy bears, shredded tissues, and a bagel with a mini-bite indentation into it. (Remarkable, thought the father-in-law, that the little yearling was served the same portion size of bagel that he was). Then came a scattering of wooden

28

blocks of assorted sizes. Then some plastic dishes from a baby kitchen set. After that came a large wet spot in the carpeting leading to an unscrewed "sippy cup" of apple juice. Everything within a six feet radius of said spill had a sticky feel to it. Following this Appalachian Trail documenting the baby's morning movements was the daughter-in-law's pocket book. It was lying on its side with its contents strewn in every direction. Like most moms' pocket books, if left unattended, it was clearly the highlight of the granddaughter's day camp activities this morning prior to the arrival of her grandparents. To the great fortune of the newest heir (after all, now that she was named after a prophetess, she was surely to go through life with great fortune), she discovered the powder and puff which her mother had failed to screw tightly shut. The powder seemed to smell so good, and it instantly was able to decorate everything reachable in the area including said granddaughter's hair and eyebrows. What a find. How nice of this precious granddaughter to be so relaxed anticipating her grandparents' visit, that wallowing in her playthings needed no modification of this fun environment in preparation.

After crossing the Cheerios-saturated crunchy carpet of the living room, the mother-in-law and father-in-law had yet to see anyone alive. They poked their heads into the kitchen. That was a fatal mistake. What they saw was a caricature of a normal kitchen, an exaggeration of the worst scenario they could possibly conjure up in their heads. The two sinks, installed for religious reasons, were stacked high with dirty dishes and glasses. The linoleum floor was very sticky, and every footstep required a strong tug to pull it off the floor. An empty Cheerios box, the obvious donor of its contents to enable the cross-living room sound effect walk, lay empty on the floor. The sink faucet was dripping. A couple of two-day old used soup pots sat on the stove. On the kitchen counter were scattered breadcrumbs and a couple of dirty napkins.

"Hi, Mom and Dad!" The loving voice of the wonderful son came from the front door behind them. "Welcome to our abode. We just picked up little Chavi from her friend's birthday party next door". Behind him came the daughter-in-law carrying Chavi.

In a hesitating voice, she said, "You told us you were coming at two, a half hour from now. I'm sorry we weren't here to greet you and I'm sorry there is such a mess."

This was followed by a somewhat awkward session of small talk after which the mother-in-law and father-in-law sat down in the living room with their son to talk, while the daughter-in-law went off to the bedroom to nurse the baby.

While her husband and son sat chatting away about the stock market, the mother-in-law sat ashen. In her mind, she had endured this horrific scene every time she came in order to spend a little time with her son and granddaughter. "What is with my son?" she thought. "Doesn't he use his eyes? How can be live in such a pig sty? Wasn't he brought up in a neat house where every speck and every smudge was dealt with as soon as anyone noticed it? Isn't she home alone for hours while the baby sleeps so that mess never accumulates? How can she live in such disarray? Is this her idea of normal? Isn't she embarrassed if someone happens to walk in? Is this the woman bringing up my precious granddaughter? Is this going to be the role model for the granddaughter's home? What happens when they have two children? Are the piles of dirty dishes in the sink going to reach the ceiling? Is this what my daughter-in-law saw in her own home? Is this what my precious son was exposed to when he picked up his future wife at her house on a date? Is there any hope here?"

When she had attempted to speak to her daughter-in-law about the possibility of getting some help, her daughter-in-law snapped at her. Her daughter-in-law had zero tolerance for any of her questions, and if the questions didn't stop, she would walk right out of the room, with Chavi. It was almost as though any suggestion of a constructive nature by the mother-in-law was instantly rejected. It was not even discussed. The mother-in-law was thus in a quandary and did not know how to proceed. When she made some gentle comments to her son, while he was always polite, his first response was usually to defend his wife. When further comments continued, her son began to get uptight, so she had to back off.

"I have lost my son, my precious son," she pondered mournfully. "He is overworked and overtired. His young wife runs the household. She refuses to learn or to take advice. He is afraid of her. What can I hope for?"

She came to the conclusion that she could not improve the situation by force, or she would eventually not be welcome in her son's home. She had to settle for other alternatives, all of which were unsatisfactory. First, she could just minimize the number of visits she made there. That would reduce the pain. The disadvantage, she

31

realized, was that she would gradually estrange herself from her son and his eventual growing family. They would get to know each other's lives less and less. She would have trouble getting close with her son's children, a prospect which saddened her greatly. And most of all, she would lose <u>her</u> boy, the pride of her family.

Second, she could visit there frequently and just keep her mouth shut. This, too, was an awful choice. Our mother-in-law was always outspoken when it came to things she felt strongly about. Silence to her meant tacit approval. Furthermore, what would she do there if the baby were asleep or nursing? Would she roll up her sleeves and start cleaning? Would that be interpreted as an insult or at least a statement to her daughter-in-law? Would she offer to do some straightening up or baby sitting, or would she wait to be asked? The latter would really be difficult for her because her nature was to automatically pitch in and assist where she saw the need for it.

Third, should she make an appointment with her son and spell out the quandary she was in? Should she let him decide as to how active a role she should play? Should she use him as an agent to find out from his wife what she should or should not do? This alternative, though logical, was not entirely comfortable for her. She really was very reluctant to put her son on the spot. Would he get angry? Would her worst fear, his loving her less, possibly result? Would her son treat the whole discussion as a questioning of his choice of marriage? Would this weaken his previously unflappable love for his wife? Would he lose his temper or break down, causing his mother unfathomable guilt? Lastly, was her son capable of dealing with this dilemma? Was he aware enough? Did he know the pride and emotions of a woman to be of any help?

# The Daughter-in-Law's Version of Her Mother-in-Law's Visit

On the day of the aforementioned visit, the daughter-in-law was in bad shape. She had developed a painful mastitis infection a few days before. She had to juggle her growing baby's strong nursing demand with the difficult treatment procedures her doctor had recommended. She was constantly sore and was sleeping very poorly as a result. She spent a lot of time considering stopping the nursing, but her pre-set goal had been a few months more. This situation was making her totally out of sorts.

She had just learned that her favorite aunt has just been hospitalized with an undetermined blood infection. She was extremely attached to this aunt who was single. The latter had lived with her family for about fifteen years since the premature death of her husband soon after their marriage. The daughter-in-law was very close to this aunt and considered her a second mother. This illness threw the daughter-in-law into a great depression. She was additionally frustrated by the fact that the ill woman was in another state and would be virtually impossible to be visited.

Chavi was driving her crazy. The baby's new ability to walk was compounded by her unsatiable curiosity and endless energy. She always seemed on the verge of some great catastrophe such as falling down the stairs or choking on a grape or toy piece. The child touched everything. When any restraint was put on her, she went into a tantrum. So, at least for the present, permissiveness was the order of the day. In addition, Chavi went into mysterious allergic attacks which were frightening to her mother. The offending allergen had still not yet been determined, and with the inherent danger built in, there was great anxiety in the air as more and more foods were introduced to the baby to supplement her nursing.

Friends in the neighborhood or lack of them worried the daughter-in-law. She had always been popular in high school and college and was accustomed to considerable female sharing. Since living in this apartment, she was very frustrated. It just wasn't happening. Those her age were either busy with their own close clique of friends or were just unavailable while doing their own thing. Many of her contemporaries were working and just not around. Others had two or three kids and were so weighed down that they rarely came up for a breath of fresh air.

Her mother-in-law gave her one big headache. For starters, that woman never looked at her with unconditional warmth and approval that her mother and aforementioned aunt did. She knew that her mother-in-law didn't particularly like her, didn't approve of most everything that she was doing, and probably would be overjoyed if her son divorced her. This impression was acquired by the way her mother-in-law treated her over the past two years, and the ever-condescending way she spoke to her at their meetings. Her mother-in-law, she decided, was not her fan, despite the fact that she was attached to her favorite son. There was an air of constant criticism and disapproval. Her mother-in-law seemed to root against her. She longed to separate from her mother-in-law, but felt that it was her duty to be civil out of respect for her husband. She turned down any offers of assistance because they were always accompanied by what her mother-in-law called "constructive suggestions". The "suggestions" were mostly unacceptable, unfortunately, because they were either too old-fashioned, too personal, too long-winded, or too hinting at a criticism of the way she, the daughter-in-law, was brought up.

So she kept her distance, and she kept Chavi at a distance as well. She would have loved to have adored the older woman as a mother. She really did need help, lots of it. She yearned for approval, for love and for closeness. Instead, she felt mostly rage, and if her husband, the "family prince", so much as intimated any support for his mother, she was prepared to reflexly send him right back to her, for good.

Her mother-in-law was simply operating on a very different wave length from her. Her mother-in-law seemed too rigid to bridge the gap. She seemed incapable of putting herself in the eyes of a newly married young mother. She talked down to her. She was not kind, and she was always referring to the way she did things when she was a young mother. She was critical of the way her son was being taken care of, of how his daughter was being raised, and how the household was being managed. Was anything good in her eyes, the daughter-in-law wondered? What a sad loss of a potentially close relationship.

What should she do? In this cold war, what were her options? Like her mother-in-law at the opposite end of the pole, she weighed the various choices, all of which seemed unacceptable.

First she could separate, either by literally moving to a different city, or staying put and discouraging getting together. The opportunity for the latter was there for the taking. Her husband often worked late, and it is traditionally the woman who sets up the family's social schedule. So, overtly or covertly, she could orchestrate a very limited visitation schedule. However, she knew this would be saddening for her gentle husband who felt very close to his mother. How could she engineer, even without his noticing, a pattern which would cause him pain and distancing? In addition, on some level, she felt that Chavi deserved two grandmothers rather than one. (She couldn't believe that she was giving her mother-in-law such consideration, when she felt as badly as she did towards her). She felt that Chavi would grow up with healthier self-esteem if four grandparents adored her rather than two.

Second, she considered welcoming her mother-in-law with open arms. She could invite her over for chats, shop with her, call her for advice and call her for recipes. She could arrange Holiday get-togethers, Sabbath get-togethers, dinners out together and weekend excursions to the mall or the zoo. She manufactured an image of her mother-in-law that certainly did not exist, that of a loving, approving parent. This invented perception would be her shield, her protection from any negative comments or thoughts sent in her direction. They would thus co-exist with closeness. Her mother-in-law would in turn relish the unexpected warmth of her daughter-in-law and the frequent meetings of their families. However, as noted earlier, she was too angry at this woman to have any pretense of closeness last more than five minutes. She knew herself. She would bristle at the first put-down. She would give herself away immediately and, if she tried to bottle in her resentment, she knew that before long she would explode, and terrible things would be said between them that might cause permanent damage. This plan of action was much too risky given her strong sense of justice.

Lastly, she could enlist her husband's assistance with her dilemma. Could he speak to his mother? Could he explain to his mother the damage that his mother was doing to his loving wife's psyche? Could he ask his mother to hold her tongue, and to be more tolerant and flexible and open to new ideas? Could she pour her heart out to her hubby and share with him the great grief that his mom causes?

Or would all this backfire? Would he fall back on the Bible's commandment to honor his mother and father? Would this inadvertently cause him to turn against her, his wife? Would he explode at her for being disrespectful and end up loving her less?

Furthermore, was he capable of dealing with all this? Was he too overtired and pre-occupied to handle a heavy-duty problem between two women that he loved? Did he have the skills to ease the problem rather than add to it?

## The Generation Gap—A Great Source of Friction

Regardless of how much mother-in-law and daughter-in-law like each other and how they get along, the difference between their generations will frequently bring up potential subjects for friction between them. The two women involved might be anywhere from twenty to forty years apart in age. Despite their personalities or their awareness level or their good intentions, when it gets down to specifics, they could be light years apart. What is normal for one generation is unheard of as normal years earlier or years later.

For example, in the mother-in-law's generation, young couples almost immediately tried to have children. They rarely postponed becoming parents, and the mother-in-law could look forward to the exciting world of being a "grandma". Grandchildren were a great source of joy between mother-in-law and daughter-in-law.

Today, this is certainly not automatic. The newlyweds often focus on their respective careers, and prefer getting a dog or a couple of cats. This is not a negotiable or discussible subject, regardless of the mother-in-law's reservations or sadness, especially if she has no other grandchildren.

In 1940, probably 98% of all households had a playpen in active use. If a mother had to use the bathroom or take out the garbage or run to the front door to respond to a knock, a playpen was an instant helper, like an instant babysitter. The toddler was safe, secure and protected from accidents. In the year 2000, the word playpen is a dirty word. Physically and symbolically, it is a jail, a cruel restriction, a shutting off of freedom and exploration. It is a symbol of the selfish mentality of the previous generation. It put the mother's agenda before the child's. It gives the mother freedom at the expense of the child.

When it comes to seat belts in a car or van, ironically, almost the exact opposite is seen. In the old days, on a family trip, kids rolled around in the back seat of a car or station wagon, and had a ball. They fought. They played. They lay down and slept across the seats or on the floor. They exchanged seats if the person next to them was bothering them. They entertained themselves. They were in a joyful separate world from the adults in the front seat. In the current day of the daughter-in-law as a mother, her kids are patiently seat belted one by one. If the "click" is not heard on a belt that is difficult to close, the car will not start. There are rules of who sits where depending on age and air bags. They are strict rules as to which way the infant seat faces. Two children in one seat belt is a no-no. There is no such thing as an adult passenger casually riding holding a child on his or her lap. The aspect of safety by far overrides any reference to freedom of the child. The aspect of the convenience of the parent at the expense of the liberty of the youngster is not even a consideration.

In the mother-in-law's generation, a good mother had her children fed, bathed and put to sleep by 6 or 7 p.m. A child seen awake after that hour was a sign of a neglectful parent and certainly a threat to the child's health. The mother-in-law was very comfortable hiring a baby sitter, even from a licensed agency, to go out with her husband and other adults as soon as the sitter arrived.

For most daughters-in-law, the reverse is true. It is a threat to the child's personal and emotional safety to have it cared for by anyone other than a parent, grandparent or member of the immediate family. In 99% of the occasions where the daughter-in-law goes out with her husband in the evening, she takes her baby with her. If she sits in a restaurant with her hubby while the baby is asleep or playing with a piece of bread next to her, even at 8 or 9 p.m., she is considered a caring, attentive parent.

When the mother-in-law was a child, chances are she was not permitted to enter the living room of her home. That room was set aside for "company". She never questioned that rule. It did not seem unfair. The room was only for adults. Even the concept of a "restricted area" was never questioned. The adult and child areas of life itself were often separate. This was totally acceptable and normal. To a daughter-in-law, this whole concept is dreadful and barbaric. Maybe even a reportable abuse. Her young children may go anywhere they want, and when they want to. Her own bedroom as well as the public areas of the house are primarily for her kids' enjoyment. She could never imagine putting a visitor's needs ahead of one of her children. So if a half eaten peanut butter and jelly sandwich ends up between the cushions of the living room couch, so be it. Punishment to the perpetrator? Unthinkable. Changing a dirty diaper on the living room carpet? Why not, if it's the nearest available surface?

When the mother-in-law was a child, she learned quickly enough not to interrupt her mother if the latter were talking to an adult either with her or over the phone. Unless the house were burning down, a child had to wait for her mom to finish. Again, it was a totally comfortable rule. It did not feel restrictive. It was an acceptance that the adult world came first. When she, the child, would grow up, she would in turn acquire these rights. If she did interfere with her mother's conversation, she might expect an impatient response and even some level of reprimand.

Not so nowadays. When the mother-in-law phones her daughter-in-law for a simple chit chat or some important agenda, she can expect an entirely different scenario. If a child is awake and near the daughter-in-law, chances are that said child has never been restricted regarding interrupting its mother talking on the phone. Probably, he or she has never been even discouraged. So the mother-in-law will hear, every minute or so, her daughter-in-law saying

"What is it, honey?" followed by words of reassurance or instruction or explanation to the child. What is perfectly normal and casual to the daughter-in-law can be interpreted by the mother-in-law as rude and disrespectful, and at least discourteous. At certain times, neither can complete a sentence. If the mother-in-law is tense over something or anxious about getting someplace, this simple conversation with her daughter-in-law can be a very trying one.

The list goes on and on. The generation gap brings to the surface frequent reminders of its existence, with the accompanying potential for irritation between the parties. How it plays out depends on what is involved and how their relationship is going. Regarding the latter, if two people really like each other and are rooting for each other, then they will deflect the seriousness of their differences into a workable form so that life can go on peacefully. This is regardless of whether these two people are dealing in a business transaction or whether they are two family members conjecturing on how to decorate a room. Any two individuals are different. There are different styles. There are different ways of expressing things, different paces of doing things and different values and priorities. Where there are good emotional attachments and the desire to keep it as such, these differences are routinely dealt with. They can be eliminated or modified or muted or accepted. They can become a refreshing positive between the parties. They can be a learning situation. We all learn new things or thoughts from people we love and admire. Differences are a source of stimulation and expansion of our own agendas.

The mother-in-law and daughter-in-law relationship is quite unique. What the mother-in-law deems unacceptable in her daughter-in-law, she probably would have no problem accepting when it comes to her own daughter. With a daughter, under normal circumstances, a child she conceived, bore, diapered and brought up, she is dealing with her own flesh and blood. Her daughter is an extension of herself. A mother-in-law will instinctively nurture her daughter every day she is on this earth. She will always love her, even when they disagree, fight, misinterpret what the other says, or when her daughter interrupts a phone call frequently to tend to a nearby child. A mother-in-law's own daughter may have significant differences from her in parenting methods, religious practice, cooking, dealing with friends, decorating, school selection and recreation priorities. However, this is her lifetime baby and any emotional separation will rarely happen.

The daughter-in-law gets no such priority acceptance of everything she does or says from her mother-in-law. She is someone else's child. She is a stranger brought into the family, the result of a son's selection methods. Maybe not quite, but she starts from scratch. She has to earn the love, closeness, enjoyment and high rank that the mother-in-law's daughter gets automatically the day she is born. She certainly may very well get up to that high rung, but in most cases, she has to work hard to get there unless there is instant chemistry between mother-in-law and daughter-in-law. The daughter-in-law will have to prove that all her mother-in-law's fears and reservations were unfounded and temporary.

Likewise, to the daughter-in-law, her mother-in-law will never, ever be her mother. Except for giving birth to the man she chose to marry, her mother-in-law is a stranger to get to know and to be dealt with. She is distant, preachy and intolerant. In addition, the difference of their age compounded by their different histories will be an enormous hurdle to overcome. Every visitation and every conversation will be a reminder of how separate their vantage points are.

The fact that they were born decades apart will in itself slow their connection on a daily basis. The prognosis, though, is good, fortunately, because human beings are by nature adaptable, and their desire to achieve closeness will overcome their built-in age gap.

## Quotes From a Mother-in-Law
## That Immediately Irritate Her Daughter-in-Law

1)   Did I wake you? (asked at 9 a.m.)

2)   Where is your playpen?

3)   Where is his other sock?

4)   Why does your husband look so thin?

5)   My kids were walking at this age.

6)   If you were a wise girl, you would…

7)   Is there a napkin in this house?

8)   How did she get that bruise on her head?

9)   Did you learn to do it that way from your mother?

10)   How come the kids are up so late?

11)   You never heard of a "children's dining room"?

12)   Why is she always barefoot?

13)   Did you ever hear of a baby sitter?

14)   You mean you don't have another set of keys?

15) Did they wash their hands with soap before they sat down to eat?

16) Why is the floor so sticky?

17) I was in the area, so instead of calling, I decided to just pop in.

18) My son is still paying off your school loan?

19) Who's taking these pre-natal vitamins?

20) How do you see through these windows?

## Quotes From A Daughter-In-Law
## That Immediately Irritate Her Mother-In-Law

1) I always toss pennies away. Who needs clutter?

2) We've decided to name the baby after a flower we both like.

3) I didn't have time to do a wash.

4) Your son said that you used to burn all your food.

5) We always go barefoot.

6) The baby will let you know when she wants to go to sleep.

7) Who said that socks have to match?

9) Your own daughters never do that!

10) Can you please take off your shoes when you come into my house?

11) I don't want my kids fat like yours are.

12) Where did your son learn such poor eating manners?

13) Please don't get me any more perfume. I think we have very different tastes.

14)    (Asked of a child age 1-100) "Would you like to go to sleep now?"

# Pre-Marital Counseling for
# Mother-in-Law and Daughter-in-Law

It is obvious that pre-marital counseling is very helpful for both mother-in-law and daughter-in-law to prepare them for their inevitable conflict. Hopefully, it will ease the expected pain that must take place between them.

Before going into the possible schedule and logistics of this counseling, the situations for each of the parties must be reviewed, for after all, they are coming from very, very different directions.

The daughter-in-law is the younger of the two rivals. She is generally young and inexperienced in life's complications. For example, she may or may not know how to cook. She may or may not have experienced a sexual relationship. She may have dated extensively before meeting THE SON, or may have dated very little due to many factors such as shyness, being very young, intense school pressures, heavy family obligations, or the lack of eligibles in her

51

home town. In fact, as in some cases, the son may have been her first date. She may be an orphan and brought up by relatives; or the opposite, having a child-like dependency on her mother and father. She may have a good support system of siblings and friends, or may be an only child with no close friend. She might have siblings who are much older or who have moved far away. She could be the only child of remarried parents with their own older children. There is every different possibility.

This young lady might be very put together, with a fine sense of self and self-esteem; or she could be struggling along and barely surviving, with very little self-confidence. She might be highly organized and functional, or somewhat scatter-brained and dependent on others to function on a daily basis.

In terms of her motivation towards getting engaged and soon to be married, again there are endless variations. This girl, coming with the history of any of the above situations, might have simply fallen head over heels in romantic love with THE SON, and this all-powerful intoxication is the only thing she is aware of in her life right now. She might, on the other hand, be making a commitment to marry because of pressure to do so by her parents, or as a variation of the latter, she might be the last of a group of friends to marry and rather than be an outcast, she is attaching to the first decent young man who seems attracted to her.

She might be marrying to attach to his extended family which she lacks because of coming from a broken home. She might be marrying for financial security as a highest priority, whether that is sometimes preached to her by her parents or learned the hard way by growing up in a family with financial instability. She might have gotten engaged because custom in her community or religious sect mandated a particular appropriate age to start a family, and she was automatically conforming with that which was expected of her.

Her future husband's profession or training might have attracted her. For example, she might have always dreamed of marrying a doctor or movie maker or professional painter. (Different strokes for different folks—no pun intended.) She might have just lost a best friend or parent or dog, and felt a terrible sense of loss and loneliness.

She might be getting older and worrying about her biological clock and the risk of having "old eggs". This, coupled with an intense desire to have children, may have stimulated her to finally go to events for singles to meet her future mate.

The bottom line of all the above is that a young woman entering into marriage is at the threshold of her adult life. She has probably finished most of her school or training, has probably weaned herself from her nuclear family, has gradually separated from high school and/or college relationships, and has stored up the amount of emotional and psychological strength that her childhood has provided for her. She has elected to proceed to her future roles of wife, mother, and possibly grandmother.

Highest on her priorities at this time, probably, are her future husband, his extended family, her future apartment or house, the family she has grown up in, children, her career, and her own maturing as a person. Her future mother-in-law in this hierarchy of priorities, is somewhere at the bottom or in the middle. This young lady, the daughter-in-law, is about to step into real adulthood. She probably wants to be the best wife ever and the best mother there ever was. In between, she herself is growing up and she probably wants to be the finest person possible.

Her first step is to be a first-class wife. Her schooling so far in this area, has been her conscious and subconscious observation of her parents' marriage, with the automatic checklist of which aspects of this marriage she wants to learn from, and which aspects to discard. She may have had the opportunity to absorb the positives and negatives of other marriages, including those of siblings, other relatives, and close friends.

She may have taken courses in school addressing skills in any relationship, such as communication, listening, expressing feelings and addressing expectations. She may have done reading on her own, drawing from the countless volumes written on marriage. She may have been fortunate to have taken courses actually preparing one for marriage. Lastly, she, with or without her future husband, may have gone for private pre-marital counseling, usually an expensive option for a young couple.

Pre-marital counseling for her, even if she is blessed with a skilled psychotherapist, has enormous ground to cover. It will assist her with her own sense of self. It will cover the expectations and unwritten contracts of marriage partners. It will review the graphic reality of living with another human up close on a daily basis, which in itself is a shocking initiation into marriage. It will review the communicative skills—listening, expressing one's self, sharing feelings, dealing with disappointments, dealing with conflicts, coping with the odd habits of a roommate, and problem solving. It might cover the business side of marriage, such as budgets, religious compromise, recreation priorities, charity giving, sharing of household duties, and who keeps the remote control.

Somewhere, on the bottom of this complicated list, sits the counseling needed for a daughter-in-law to recognize and deal with her new mother-in-law. A wise therapist will not overlook this classic battle amidst all the other ground she has to cover on her agenda. The therapist has to more or less define a mother-in-law to this relatively inexperienced young woman. She must teach the latter where a mother-in-law is coming from, why the older woman automatically has a problem with her, and why even the best individuals are subject to this conflict.

She must teach the new wife that even though her relationship with her mother-in-law is by far less important than the other huge priorities confronting her, she <u>must</u> do well in this new relationship. Otherwise, it will be an almost daily irritant in her married life, especially if her husband chooses to stay closely connected with his parents.

Her mother-in-law does have a built in status that has to be recognized. She is, after all, the mother of the beloved husband. She will, by definition, be a grandmother to any children of the daughter-in-law. She will be, because of her attachment to her son and/or grandchildren, a potentially frequent visitor to the household. She will, by definition, have strong opinions about how said son and/or grandchildren are being taken care of by said daughter-in-law. She will, by extension, judge her daughter-in-law as a person as well as a relative, by her perception of how this care is delivered. As an experienced homemaker, the mother-in-law will judge the daughter-in-law's specific abilities such as the daughter-in-law's choice of the décor and furnishings, as well as the neatness and cleanliness of the house. As an experienced mother, she will judge the parenting skills of her young daughter-in-law. With both being wives and caretakers of households, they are frequently in a situation where they judge each other, more so, for example, than a daughter-in-law and her father-in-law.

The therapist must remind the daughter-in-law that the mother-in-law, being older and perceiving herself as wiser as result, will feel comfortable judging her daughter-in-law in many areas. This the mother-in-law would never do so freely with friends of her own age group. The therapist must remind the daughter-in-law that the mother-in-law perceives of her son as the best catch in creation, someone who could have any great girl in the whole world. She, the daughter-in-law, will constantly be inspected and analyzed and graded to confirm that she was indeed worthy of being the final selection of THE SON. The counselor must show the daughter-in-law that to live up to her mother-in-law's critical eye, subjectively or objectively, is an almost impossible task.

Finally, the counselor, after explaining the background and inevitability of this classic conflict, must review the various strategies of deflecting the frequent pain. Unlike other people in her life who irritate her, the mother-in-law cannot be avoided. The mother-in-law's potential for causing trouble cannot be discounted. (In most other relationships, we surround ourselves with people who love us and value us, and we stay far, far away from those individuals who resent us or make us feel not so good about ourselves.) She is here to stay. The daughter-in-law, with proper therapy, can master the techniques and strategies that will not only soothe the bad times but have the potential of making the two of them close, even good friends. Human beings, as impaired as they are by the powerful emotions they are created with, have great potential to soar high. They are built with a basic goodness and great flexibility. With patient instruction and encouragement, they can be softened, be molded and be scolded into a higher level than they began, and this is the reason that the prognosis in the mother-in-law - daughter-in-law conflict is good to great.

Pre-marital counseling for the mother-in-law? Her first reaction would be <u>never</u> in a thousand years! After all, she is older. She is wiser. She has earned her stripes. She has paid her dues. She perceives of herself as a veteran of many battles which have given her the wisdom she finally feels. After twenty-five years or so of marriage, she has civilized and tamed and patiently educated her wild stallion of a husband, which was no easy feat. After twenty-five or so years running a home with its myriad problems, she finally has a system that works. She has worked tremendously hard with decorating, with repairs and innovations, and with kids' messes; and now she is the master of a smoothly running machine. She has raised her three children with great personal sacrifice, surviving so many episodes and crises which brought her grief and anguish. She took courses, read copiously and networked frequently in order to give her kids the best that was in her power to give. She juggled a job and mothering, often with great tension, to make things work for the family.

Finally, finally, she pushed her busy, shy son into agreeing to date. She put her whole heart into the effort. She privately was crushed every time he was <u>not</u> interested in girls that she knew of as being both lovely and well put-together. Her beloved son finally made his selection. He chose someone <u>so</u> different from that which she imagined, so far removed from the type of classmates and friends that he had so much fun with during all his school years.

To deal with this stranger, she, the worn workhorse, needed therapy? That will be the day!

In truth, though, she <u>does</u> need some kind of professional guidance. Why? Because nothing in her life experience, (even another daughter-in-law!) can prepare her for this classic mother-in-law—daughter-in-law struggle. All her wisdom, all her experience, all her insight, all of her joy of her son's engagement after such a long wait—all of these cannot get her over the hump of this special conflict.

Her daughter-in-law cannot be overpowered. It won't work! She cannot be threatened. She cannot be taken out of the will. She cannot be insulted behind the back of THE SON. She cannot be paid off to disappear. She cannot be tip toed around. Until she is ready, she cannot be taught. She cannot be bullied by THE SON's siblings. She cannot be given the silent treatment. The DIL cannot be made into an MIA.

Despite her youth and experience, she has a rank and status which cannot be yanked from her. First and foremost, THE SON loves her! Any grief to THE SON is like a stab in the heart. Second, the daughter-in-law runs the household in which THE SON resides. Anything seen or heard or going on in this household, theoretically at least, has the son's approval. Third, the daughter-in-law is the future mother of the grandchildren that will carry the family name. No, these grandchildren cannot have just one parent, your son. They must have two, which includes the daughter-in-law. So, whether one likes it or not, these children who unfortunately will probably look like their mother's side of the family, will be brought up in _her_ home, eating _her_ food, wearing clothes _she_ bought, repeating values _she_ taught, and spending time with those relatives that _she_ likes. Now, all of this is a lot of power for a young whippersnapper to wield.

So, the middle-aged mother-in-law, does truly, after all, need help to deal with this new lump in her throat. She, who has survived many of life's traumas with sweat and integrity and persistence and good judgment, now needs therapy for the first time in her life. Her presenting problem? A new relationship that she has never run into before, despite all her years.

This assistance, now in terms of traditional therapy, will possibly eventually become commonplace and even a requirement. It will soon raise no more eyebrows than going to a dermatologist to cure a persistent rash. The help can be actual therapy, visiting a psychotherapist for a series of sessions. It could be in the form of group therapy, whereby mothers-in-law would sign up for a series of sessions led by a trained leader. At these sessions, they would share their stories, their frustrations, their disappointments and their perceived woes. By listening to others, they would have their pain eased. They would pick up pointers given by those getting pretty good at the relationship. Initially, though, one would expect great relief and laughing and applause, as every participant listens in disbelief, hearing with great joy that others have the identical problem.

The goal, as far away it seems, is at least co-existence and hopefully a closer friendship between the adversaries. Again, the prognosis is good to great. The mother-in-law will learn to have patience with her new daughter-in-law, the same patience she used raising her own children. The mother-in-law will recognize the insecurity of this new wife and caretaker of the home, and allow for learning mistakes as she would allow anyone else. She would value this young woman as someone bringing quiet warmth and happiness to her son. She will try to smooth the transition of this daughter-in-law, someone else's child, into her own family, as a new daughter.

Pre-marital therapy, the daughter-in-law—mother-in-law variety, would thus save months or even years of avoidable pain. It is hoped that the psychotherapy profession and the spiritual leaders will recognize its being a vital part of preparation for new marriages, not just a tangential aside.

The bottom line is a double benefit. First, the three generations of grandmother, mother and children will have a smooth relationship, giving all involved years and years of family warmth and support, as well setting up the proper role models for future generations. Second, the marriage in question itself will be much stronger if the partners don't have to deal with an outside irritation that is for the most part avoidable. There is a huge amount of pressure as it is, and having a loving mother-in-law—daughter-in-law relationship would be a delightful assistance in helping this fledgling family grow.

The prognosis, again, is good to excellent.

# The Key Ingredient: How Does the Young Couple Get Along?

The primary role of a newlywed young woman is that of a wife and romantic object of her new husband. She is also a brand new homemaker. Soon after, if blessed, she has the awesome responsibility of being a new mother. These are all new identities in most cases, and a huge emotional load for anyone.

Her new husband, THE SON, is her future in the long life ahead of her. He is committed to being her source of love and emotional support. In addition, he is a fledgling financial supporter of the family, a partner in running the home, and an upcoming Daddy to their future offspring.

How close this married couple becomes will usually determine the skill and the joy they will experience in these new difficult roles.

How well do they score on the essential ingredients of a marriage? Is the communication between the two working and effective? Can each express feelings? Are they aware of their feelings? Do they know the words that can best describe them? For example, rather than "I feel good" or "I had a good day" which convey a general feeling of well-being, more specific adjectives tell much more. "I am relieved. I am proud. I am content. I am excited. I feel loved. My work is appreciated. My work was noticed. My efforts were validated! I am so grateful." Likewise, do the marital partners stop at "I had a awful day" or "I feel lousy" or do they go further? "I am very nervous. I am ashamed. I am frightened. Something is really worrying me. I feel unappreciated. I am feeling lonesome. Why do I feel neglected?"

Have they learned the extremely difficult skill of listening? Listening, at best, is a lost art. Very few individuals are capable. Most of us are so busy in our minds with our own heavy agenda of feelings and activities that we quickly tune out a speaker as soon as the speaker says something which reminds us of an item on our agenda. The speaker promptly loses us when a strong personal concern or emotion reflexly kicks in. A listener needs to be mighty secure within his or her own skin to empathize with the speaker's message.

Furthermore, can the listener hear the emotion of the one speaking which lies behind the verbal message? The words often veil the actual communication. A husband steps into his front door after a long work day, takes a long whiff, shuts the door behind him and yells out to his wife in the kitchen, "Are we having meat loaf again tonight? It must be the third time this week!" If his wife is not skilled in "active" listening, that is hearing the message behind the message, she will blunder badly by responding defensively. "If you don't like what we're having, why don't you eat at your favorite tavern where they'll feed you what you want. Don't do me any favors and shut the door behind you."

A wise wife with better listening skills immediately senses that something is upsetting her usually pleasant partner. She knows that he is usually quite hungry when he arrives home, and will ordinarily devour anything a foot by a foot by a foot set before him. If he had meat loaf seven days a week, he would scarcely notice. She will respond more appropriately with "You really had a bad day." Or, "You really sound upset." She will rush to greet him with warmth and patience, and soon he will settle down and, without too much coaxing, will reveal what actually happened that threw him for a loop. The result is a close sharing and reassurance about a bad experience.

Lastly, a wise insight comes from the question. "What is the opposite of speaking?" Unfortunately, in most cases, the answer is not "listening" Rather, it is "waiting to speak," a sad commentary on the scarcity of skilled communication between individuals.

How about other marriage essentials? Do husband and wife thank each other <u>every</u> day for something that the other has done for them? There is always something, even in busy households, like her folding up his sweaters, or his stopping at the post office to get her stamps. Do they each show affection daily? Forgetting about intimacy, there must be constant hugging, kissing and touching. Do they compliment each other regularly? "Your hair looks really terrific." or "You're really doing better with Junior these days." or "You make me feel very proud of you."

Do they ply each other with gifts on a regular basis, that is, besides the usual birthday and anniversary ones? A close couple "think gifts" on an ongoing basis, picking up some kind of treat for the other regardless of the source. It could be a little trinket from a gift shop or a great magazine from a newsstand or some great note paper while at a stationer ordering business forms. It could simply be an unsolicited hot potato knish—anything that brings out a smile and says "I was thinking of you today, honey."

Are they compassionate when their mate is having trouble with a sibling or a friend? Are they patient and interested and actively helpful when a particular relationship is having problems? Are they able to "agree to disagree" on issues where they see things differently from one another? Can they conclude those discussions still "liking" each other without anger or tension?

Do they patiently discuss other aspects of marriage that impact their mates and have to be worked out? How much charity to give out annually? To whom? Which schools are better for their children? Which neighborhood to live in? How much money to budget for trips and recreation? Do they set aside a certain time every week, fixed in stone, to be alone with each other, away from kids, computers, friends and relatives, remote controls, and telephones? This could be a meal at a restaurant on a particular night with the site preferably out of their neighborhood to minimize the chance of running into someone they know. It could be a certain afternoon that both are available from work, and if there are children, a baby sitter is available. If they are very fortunate, they can have a midweek overnight rendezvous to run off to. The key here is that <u>quantity</u> time, not just quality time, is absolutely essential in order for two people to really get to know one other. And after years and years of this investigation, this "alone time" gives the rare opportunity to ask one's mate "How goes it, honey? What are you working on? What are you thinking about? Tell me about your dreams." It is incomprehensible that such a protected time as this is not set aside in most marriages.

Being loved fills us with the emotional fuel and good feeling to give love to others. Receiving emotionally and materially enables us to reach out and give to other individuals. If husband and wife seek every opportunity to give to one another on a regular basis, they will be secure and deeply content as individuals and as a unit. They in turn will have the strength to be generous of heart as their world expands and they mature.

In the context of the mother-in-law—daughter-in-law relationship, how happy and secure the daughter-in-law is in her marriage will dictate the tone of how they get along. On the assumption that the mother-in-law's opinions, suggestions, judgments, values and living style will be a constant diet heard loudly by her daughter-in-law, the latter's responses will be strongly impacted by how she feels about the husband, THE SON. For example, if THE SON is not a particularly loving or attentive husband, his wife will not be a happy camper. She will probably overreact to her mother-in-law's overtures and even her presence, and her responses will be exaggerated inappropriateness. In addition, she will see her husband as starting to act and talk like his mother, and she will be most willing to return him to the womb or at least back to the mother that he takes after. She will be hostile to her mother-in-law at every opportunity, even if this reaction is totally out of context. The mother-in-law will not be able, on her own, to improve their interaction because she is dealing with an angry, discontented adversary.

Conversely, if the married young couple are two peas in a pod, two chirping lovebirds, working together both in sync and in sink (!), the mother-in-law—daughter-in-law pair have a better future together. The daughter-in-law will consider her mother-in-law as the woman who created the son that she adores and that adores her. She will make allowances for the older woman's intolerances and uncomfortable suggestions. She will instinctively treat her mother-in-law with the automatic respect and diplomacy she would give any elder. She will make the extra effort to respond to her mother-in-law's requests and needs, and feel that she is pleasing her husband at the same time.

While it is possible for a young lady to be madly in love with her husband and, at the same time hate his mother, this scenario is quite improbable. And if it is so, the anger will gradually be muted in time.

The mother-in-law had better pray that the training she gave the boy she raised will produce a great husband. The SON's skills in pleasing his wife will be a huge factor in the mother-in-law—daughter-in-law prognosis.

# Can a Mother-in-Law Damage Her Son's Marriage?

The answer to the above is arguable. There are probably three common scenarios set up by the <u>stated</u> disapproval by a mother of her son's choice of wife, while her son is still single, leading to different paths.

Firstly, if a young man is smitten by a woman, if he loves the touch of her and the sight of her and it makes him alive as he has never experienced before, he will probably overrule his mother's plea to reconsider, and push on to marry his beloved. Now this overruling, depending on the mother-son relationship, might be slow and polite with many analytical discussions and dialog. It might, on the other hand, cause an angry rift between mother and son with regrettable words spoken and very emotional outbreaks. Most male lovers will be protective of their selected women, and will relentlessly proceed to marriage. If he comes from a close family, he will, after asserting himself here, hope that his family will sooner or later get over their negative attitude, and come to realize how special his bride is. He will passionately feel that it is his life to live, and he will never meet a girl so lovely and perfect even if he searches forever. He knows intellectually that everyone's taste is different, that many of his friends are married to girls whom their family disapproves of, and that things turn out okay. His mother, whose judgement he always relied on during his long upbringing, is unfortunately unaware, he perceives, of the treasure he has been blessed with. His mother will always adore him, and in time, will come around and get to love his new wife. In summary, in this case, the son persists with his selection despite his family's reservations. He is confident. Everything will work out, he explains to his new wife. The marriage partners proceed forward with love and normal momentum, and have a good chance as any to have a long, loving relationship.

A second scenario sees the son relenting under pressure from his mother. Over the years, he has grown accustomed to listening to his mom's opinions. He trusts her values and judgement. He is ever confident that she has his well-being at heart. She wants the best for him. She has life experience. She has never let him down. She knows instinctively what is not good for him. He ends the relationship, as difficult as it might be. He can live with this decision. Once his mom has planted a serious question about his choice, the young woman in question doesn't look the same anymore, anyway. He cannot envision a future married to an individual that his mother is not crazy about. He sees a long life in the future. He does not want to lose the comfort and closeness of the family that has given him a lifetime of security.

The third possibility is the most problematic one. Here the son cannot confidently choose one of the above two options. Rather, he compromises, trying to please everyone. On one hand, he cannot let go of the girl he is so attracted to. She has her trust in him. Once she knew how much he loved her, she became ecstatic about her new man, and she became dependent on his love. They have grown accustomed to one another. They laugh together. They dream together. They have made plans about what their future life together would be like. They are both on a high. Even hinting that all this might come to an end would be devastating for her. He would be violating a trust. This precious girl, starved for love until she met him, would be thrown away to fend for herself? No, this was definitely not an option to him. On the other hand, he has really never cut the cord from his mother. Whether he be an underdeveloped "mama's boy" or simply genuinely attached to his nuclear family, he cannot envision a lifetime separated from them. They represent security. They are his roots. They represent the "womb" from whence he came.

So he proceeds into a marriage flawed from the beginning. His mother and probably his father are in great pain over his overriding their vote. He sees it in their eyes. He easily senses their lack of enthusiasm over the new member in the family. He knows what they are like when they really get excited about someone. He looks at his new wife with a jaundiced eye. She cannot be as great as he imagined if he never got his mother's blessing. Although he proceeds with the proper progress of a newlywed husband, he has a constant deep pain. He does not have a full loving heart in any direction now. He easily sees the friction between his mom and his wife at family get-togethers. And, if there is no visible friction, it could be worse. There could be that polite distance between them, just a chilly co-existence. He is doomed from the start.

The prognosis here? It could go either way. It will probably get better. If he is wise enough to live some distance away from his disapproving parents early in his marriage, he has a decent chance of solidifying his closeness with his wife. Over the years, many factors will help to bring his mother and wife back together to the level of warmth he always had hoped for—initial separation of the two individuals, mellowing, getting accustomed to the differences between one another, children, and, unfortunately sometimes, illness.

# The Daughter-in-Law's Mother—The Lady or the Tiger?

In the eyes of the mother-in-law, the true villain behind all her suffering is her daughter-in-law's mother. It is the latter that not only is the probably principal role model in the daughter-in-law's life, but the actual flesh and blood person who brought her up from the day she was born.

In the mother-in-law's struggle with her new daughter-in-law, one haunting question keeps repeating itself. Where, oh where, did my daughter-in-law learn to do what she does, think what she thinks, value what she values, say what she says, and respond as she responds. Intellectually, the mother-in-law, in her forties or fifties, is aware that a newlywed woman is not only inexperienced in marriage and housekeeping and parenting, but she is "wet behind the ears" in terms of life itself. Beginner mistakes are to be expected. Naivety in dealing with business people is natural at this age. Relationships with adults is still a new area to be refined.  Parenting is often learned by trial and error.  However, a mother-in-law, shocked over what her daughter-in-law just did or said inappropriately, cannot help reacting with great anguish, cursing the <u>source</u> of the nonsense she has just witnessed.

If the new apartment of her son and his wife is a hopeless mess, and continues, even at relaxed time, to remain a mess, she will conclude that her daughter-in-law was brought up in a mess, and is very comfortable in such an environment.  It is, after all, the woman of the house who cleans and vacuums and launders and determines the cleanliness quotient of the living quarters.  If the daughter-in-law comes up with an incredible theory as to what is healthy for her toddler child to eat, which defies all logic and available information, her mother-in-law knows she must be parroting some weird teaching she got from her mother who fed <u>her</u> as a child.  If her daughter-in-law is super neurotic about germs and toxic vapors that her new baby is exposed to, to the point where she will keep said baby more or less locked up in limited quarters and away from any normal breathing child or adult to an extreme degree, the mother-in-law is convinced that she knows where this nuttiness came from.

If the daughter-in-law is perceived as simply lazy, and the mother-in-law sees her son doing everything for his wife after a long day's work and exhausting himself in the process, the mother-in-law will be after the neck of her "machatenista", her daughter-in-law's mother.  And, on top of this, if her precious son gets sick or even out of sorts as a result, we know the person on the top of the mother-in-law's hit list.

When the mother-in-law, in the throes of her disenchantment with her daughter-in-law, does meet up with the latter's mother, what does she actually see in this person? Naturally, it varies. The mother could be an older twin of the daughter-in-law, talking the same, responding the same, even laughing the same. The mother-in-law would then immediately identify this woman as the enemy and the cause of it all. She would distance herself from this woman to prevent an inevitable explosion between the two. Similar distancing, because of the son and children involved, cannot be protectively practiced, obviously, with her daughter-in-law.

On the other hand, to her shock, the mother-in-law might find her daughter-in-law's mother to be a lovely person—warm, intelligent and aware. Shrugging her shoulders, the mother-in-law might attribute her own bad luck to good genes skipping a generation. Maybe, furthermore, that would herald great hopes for the grandchildren! This would be some consolation for the suffering she is forced to endure.

The questions comes up—is this identification of a perceived villain, the mother who bore and raised the daughter-in-law that brings her mother-in-law so much grief, helpful to the situation or not? Probably, in some cases, it is good. In some cases, it makes no difference.

If the mother-in-law is one of those people who feels less upset if something bad happens to her because of something she cannot control, then having the existence of a villain is very comforting. "My daughter-in-law is a sweet girl, with very good intentions. What can I expect if she comes from a mother like that? Hopefully, with better influence around her as she matures, I have great optimism for her and our future relationship."

If the existence of an identified villain sheds no comfort on the unhappy mother-in-law, nothing will change. Until, hopefully, natural processes create a closer tie with her son's wife, she will struggle in despair. She will shout in pain or suffer silently. She will seek comfort with contemporaries who are in a similar bind, or go at it alone. Until the sun shines again, what will be her ongoing motto? "The apple never falls far from the tree."

# The Daughter-In-Law's Relationship with Her Own Mother

While it is obvious that everyone entering adulthood and marriage is the product of years of influence and baggage and relationships, one influence, in particular, stands out when we consider the mother-in-law—daughter-in-law syndrome. How did the daughter-in-law and her mother get along? How close were they? Is her mother alive? When the daughter-in-law is testing the waters of her involvement with a new mother-in-law, what role is her natural mother playing? Is she nearby? Is she available for assistance, for advice and for babysitting? Is she currently in the picture, or distracted by significant things going on elsewhere in <u>her</u> life. How is her health? Were they close when the daughter-in-law was growing up? Was the daughter-in-law's family full of siblings and even live-in older relatives so that she got lost in the shuffle? Or perhaps she was an only child with an extraordinary amount of attention focused on her. Did her mother work full time so that the daughter-in-law, for the most part, fended for herself and was self taught in many areas? By extension, in the latter case, did the daughter-in-law get accustomed to networking with her own peers and friends on issues that came up, rather than turn to older adults for instruction and feedback? Or, rather, was her mother a full time mom who was leaned on frequently for affection, for wisdom and for guidance?

There are more questions. Was the daughter-in-law in question an oldest child, which brings to a great majority a sense of independence and strong personality? Or was she the baby of the family—coddled, babied, indulged and protected? Perhaps she was an angry or at least lonely, neglected middle child?

Did the daughter-in-law grow up amidst a large extended family with aunts and uncles and cousins and grandparents constantly around? The assumption in such a case, is that older adults were familiar, were friendly, and for sure, were on her side. Conversely, was the family tiny, or at least with very few nearby relatives, so that the adult related world of the daughter-in-law consisted of her father and her mother?

Furthermore, by extension, how did her mother treat <u>her</u> in-laws, her father's parents? Did she witness her mother's closeness with her mother-in-law and did she grow up thinking that such closeness was the expected thing? Or, perhaps the grandparents were not alive or lived far away. Or, perhaps there <u>was</u> a relationship and a bad one, and she, the child, was not shielded from the squabbling or bad-mouthing.

There are many more questions and many, many more variables. The point is that a young woman marrying into a family, as inexperienced and immature as she appears, is not coming from a vacuum. She may think she is totally neutral and that her future relationship with her new mother-in-law starts on a clean slate, but this is definitely not so. On the contrary, one could argue that what will transpire is mostly pre-set and really predictable. If analyzed extensively, one could argue that the mother-in-law's nature and personality could be any type, and the daughter-in-law would still relate in the same way.

If, therefore, a good or a bad beginning is foretold, at least from the daughter-in-law's vantage, and this process is all natural and expected, then if the relationship has to be changed from its pre-cast die, it will need an enormous effort on the part of the principals to reverse the reality of what it is.

Returning to the original question of the influences of the daughter-in-law's relationship with her own mother on the mother-in-law—daughter-in-law bond, let us review some of the possibilities. For starters, if the daughter-in-law is very close with her mother, where they are affectionate with each other, enjoy each other and frequently share with each other, if this mother is healthy and available and nearby, this closeness will predictably continue into the daughter-in-law's married life. Regardless of how wonderful her new mother-in-law might be, and how generous the latter is with her time, attention, and money, a close natural mother comes first. Probably, in this case, the daughter-in-law will treat her natural mother as she did before marriage, that is powerfully attached, while her mother-in-law will, at best, be attached to her in a cordial and polite way, respectful but distant. All this is good and normal providing the mother-in-law is not looking for more. If the mother-in-law attempts to adopt her as another child on a par with the mother-in-law's natural children, she is in for a disappointment. At best, the daughter-in-law will treat her as she would any relative of her new husband, like an aunt or cousin. It would take time and life changes, even under ideal circumstances, for the daughter-in-law to get really close to her mother-in-law while her own mother is available.

If the daughter-in-law has a poor relationship with her own mother, or the latter is not well or rarely around, two strong possibilities will arise. Either the daughter-in-law, when she gets married, might be desperate for a mother figure which she is missing, and rush to bond with her new husband's mother. Or, she might lump all older female parents into one category, all negative, and not care for any of them, and in the process, reject a solicitous new mother-in-law.

The first possibility is more to be expected. A new bride that lacks a tight bond with her own mother will probably grab the opportunity to replace this void by attaching to her new mother-in-law. This need would be good for both. An affectionate, needy, interested daughter-in-law is a blessing to any mother-in-law, regardless of what else is going on in her life. It would instantly bring out the nurturing instincts that a mother feels for a child seeking her out. In fact, this new warmth would go a long way toward obliterating all the vast differences between the two in style of living and values that cause the mother-in-law—daughter-in-law problem in the first place. A good hug and smile in greeting a mother-in-law when the latter visits easily blunts the natural amazement the mother-in-law has over the incredible mess that she sees in her daughter-in-law's home. The daughter-in-law would be treated more like a daughter. She would be privy to her mother-in-law's confidence. She would get the important ranking of a member of the nuclear family. If she is criticized by her opinionated mother-in-law, it would be with her best interest at heart, rather than with the underlying resentment that many mothers-in-law harbor.

The second possibility, where the daughter-in-law automatically lumps her new mother-in-law into the same category as her own mother whom she dislikes, gives the mother-in-law—daughter-in-law relationship, at least from the daughter-in-law's perspective, a very poor start. The daughter-in-law might see all older women as critical, judgmental, intolerant, cold, self-centered, and hopelessly out of touch with the current generation. The daughter-in-law is weary of hearing how they did things in the old days; how if she were a <u>wise</u> child, she would follow established and traditional ways of doing things. If she were a <u>wise</u> child, she would not be so permissive with her children. If she were a <u>wise </u>child, she would see to it that her husband, THE SON, visited more. If she were a wise child, <u>she </u>would determine what is good for a child to be eating, not to leave it in the judgement of a two-year-old, etc, etc.

The daughter-in-law is just sick and tired of being told what to do, where to be, what to say, how to dress, and what to feel. She is weary of being judged from head to toe at every meeting or visit. She has had her fill as to how messy her kitchen is and how her living room floor is a safety hazard. Until things change, this daughter-in-law will spend most of her time with her own contemporaries who share the growing pains with her. She will minimize her contact with her mother-in-law, on any of many contexts, to simply spare herself of unneeded aggravation and disapproval.

In summary, much of the mother-in-law—daughter-in-law relationship is pre-programmed before the two principals meet each other for the first time. Each is at a time of life filled with positive and negative anticipation, such that their expectations here are for the most pre-ordained. The actual individuals filling the role are arguably incidental. If either the daughter-in-law or mother-in-law were replaced by another, what follows could very well be near the same. The expectations before the fact, good and bad, are in place.

So, how a mother relates to her daughter growing up in her household will greatly influence how this daughter will fare with the mother of the man she will marry.

# Other Daughters-in-Law in the Family

Other daughters-in-law in the family constitute a mixed bag. They can be a source of positive feeling or negative feeling. A mother-in-law—daughter-in-law duo is sometimes affected strongly by their presence or addition to the scene. Depending on what else is happening, they can further aggravate an already stressed relationship or can be a delightful, positive influence on the antagonists. Mothers-in-law and daughters-in-law are affected by additional daughter-in-laws in different ways.

To the mother-in-law, having one or more additional daughters-in-law creates a source of comparison between them. This comparison can be helpful or destructive. If the mother-in-law is having trouble with the wife of one of her sons, she will automatically look at the other daughter-in-law in the areas where the first one is giving her the most trouble. For example, if the daughter-in-law in question tends to be lazy in her housekeeping or industriousness, and if the second daughter-in-law effortlessly "does it all", the former looks twice as bad in the eyes of the mother-in-law. The diagnosis is confirmed. On the other hand, if daughter-in-law #1 plays the piano beautifully and is filling her free time with singing lessons and art courses, daughter-in-law #2, who prefers to alternate watching TV and napping, will look awfully inept. Or, if one daughter-in-law gives her mother-in-law a warm greeting and a hug every time she sees her, while her fellow daughter-in-law is a rather cold person by nature who prefers no touching, the mother-in-law obviously will feel much more comfortable with the former, and build up an unpleasant attitude toward the latter. If the mother-in-law is having a dreadful time with a daughter-in-law who is somewhat snippy or fresh whenever they get into a conversation, the arrival of a new daughter-in-law who is both very aggressive and possessing a foul mouth will make the first daughter-in-law look kind of gentle by comparison.

The mother-in-law, more or less, does benefit by having two or more daughters-in-law. She is able to see the goods and bads in each. Since most everyone has saving graces in some areas to balance the weak ones, the mother-in-law intellectually will be able to see the positive more clearly, which will serve to soften her anger or disappointment.

Secondly, for the suffering mother-in-law, another daughter-in-law will be a distraction. She will not have to instantly focus on her woes with number one. This dilution factor can be a wonderful relief. There is safety in numbers. A middle-aged mother-in-law with a lot of time on her hands can start obsessing. Her pain will make it uncomfortable for everyone around her, from her son to her children to her friends, etc. If she is forced to be busy with two or more families and certainly with any grandchildren on the scene, her primary misery will lose its exclusiveness in her thinking time. One of the best relievers of pain, oddly enough, is additional pain in a different area of the body. A split skin under a thumbnail can drive someone crazy. It usually responds to nothing and must run its course. The only thing that can make it feel better is a more annoying ache—like from a sty in the eye or a throbbing shoulder pain. Suddenly, that thumb which felt like someone was sticking a needle into it, becomes lost as the exclusive disturber of the peace. It now has competition for first place of annoyance.

Conversely, the beleaguered mother-in-law could have the opposite reaction to the above "diluted distraction" theory. She may be doing pretty well adapting to two daughters-in-law and feeling really proud of herself, when the third daughter-in-law says or does something incomprehensibly horrific. The mother-in-law falls apart. The domino theory kicks in. They all start looking bad again. "Woe is me," she wails, "what did I ever do to deserve this? I thought one was awful, but I cannot and will not handle a whole batch of misfits!" She falls back to square one, steeped in self-pity and hopelessness. She must start all over on the road uphill, knowing now that she is not strong enough to withstand the periodic setbacks that she is doomed to experience.

Another factor. If one of the daughters-in-law in a family possesses a quality or talent that the mother-in-law enjoys a lot, rather than this causing a negative comparison, it might do the opposite. It might fill the mother-in-law's need in this area and she may have a more relaxed expectation of the others, easing her disappointment.

What about the effect of other daughters-in-law, either new on the scene or preceding her, on the beleaguered daughter-in-law? As with their effect on her mother-in-law, the effect of the others on the daughter-in-law can go either way. If the daughter-in-law is having a really bad time with her mother-in-law, her ability to discuss her despair with her sisters-in-law can be very comforting. They can form a mini anti- mother-in-law club and compare notes. They can giggle together and trade stories. The one who is married longer can advise the newcomer on the former's experiences, and can describe what was helpful to her in easing the tension. She can perhaps short cut the long process of trial and error and painful learning for the newcomer. The incumbent daughter-in-law can likewise be a good amateur therapist for the newlywed. She can offer a shoulder to cry on. She can be a good listener. She could become the main confidante to her new sister-in-law, even better than the latter's own husband. After all, the men involved, often not as aware or sensitive as their wives to begin with, and frequently less helpful and patient with these problems, have another limitation. They are, after all, their mother's sons. They have known their mothers longer than they know their wives. They respect their mothers and are protective instinctively. As correct and logical as their wives recounting of their woeful run-ins and conversations are, the men, if dutiful sons, will not give their wives the validation and acknowledgement they are looking for. Hence a fellow daughter-in-law, one who has the same struggles, is frequently a more satisfying individual to share feelings with here.

However, if the daughter-in-law is unlucky, her fellow sisters-in-law can make the pain even worse. Consider the situation where the newly arriving daughter-in-law has a sister-in-law who is adored by their common mother-in-law. The latter two hug each other visibly, shop together, seek each other's advice and generally seek each other out. The mother-in-law freely offers babysitting time, takes her on shopping sprees and publicly tells people how fortunate she is that her son married such a wonderful human being. The mother-in-law crowing about one daughter-in-law and squabbling constantly with her other daughter-in-law is the ultimate nightmare for the latter.

This huge difference can be simply chemistry. Wrong or right, some women hit it off together immediately and enjoy each other, and some turn each other off. Some pairings have one making the other feel good about herself, while some make the other feel small and inadequate. Chemistry is mysterious in its ways. Where there are good vibes, it could simply be that the other consciously or subconsciously reminds them of someone else, currently or from their past, that induces strong positive feelings. For sure the reverse is equally true. One often instantly dislikes someone new who reminds them of someone they abhor for one reason or another.

It could be worse. Rather than chemistry which at least could be explained away as illogical or unfounded, the reasons a daughter-in-law sees her mother-in-law strongly preferring her sister-in-law could be based on fact. The sister-in-law could be a superior housekeeper, a superior mother, possessing infinite talents, better looking, warmer by nature, a sweeter communicator, have an unusually upbeat disposition, someone who unashamedly seeks out advice, someone who dresses her children creatively, someone who has a flair for home decorating, a great cook, and someone who couldn't wait to be married and have a mother-in-law to have a close relationship with. Wow! Any one of the above could make the average daughter-in-law feel about one foot tall and totally hopeless about any future decent relationship with her mother-in-law.

However, in <u>any</u> family, no two people are the same. Every individual has his or her strong points as well as a list of weak ones. Everyone is capable of learning and of maturing. Life is long, and nothing is forever. The apparently pitiful daughter-in-law in the above example can blossom over a period of time like anyone else. If she and her mother-in-law have the desire to do better and to become good friends, the prognosis is not as gloomy as would be apparent. As the mother-in-law and daughter-in-law get to know each other more and more, and get wiser with time, they will find a long list of things to like about the other and attain eventual closeness.

## The Role of the Respective Siblings

The siblings of the daughter-in-law and her husband have an opportunity to impact in very varied degrees on the mother-in-law—daughter-in-law difficulties.

For starters, many factors would serve to <u>minimize</u> their role:

1.  Few siblings or occasionally lack of any.

2.  Siblings much older or much younger. Not only are they far removed from empathizing with the current problem, but they are less close in general about day to day goings on and problems in the life of their brother or sister.

3.  Geographical separation, which by its nature minimizes frequent contact in busy growing families. Phone contact and occasional family holiday get-togethers barely have enough time to cover the major

topics such as new births and new maturing of the children. Individual tensions or smoldering relationships are addressed minimally or not at all.

4.    Siblings from second marriages where there is a shortened history between the members and perhaps a shortened sensitivity to individual disappointments and anxieties.

5.    Dysfunctional families where there are quite a few messed up people all over the place. With borderline individuals fighting for their own survival, there is usually not enough empathy to go around to reach out to help the next one.

However, where the new daughter-in-law <u>has</u> close siblings, especially sisters, the latter can have a major influence on the progress of the classic daughter-in-law—mother-in-law conflict.

Firstly, if the new bride has a close sister, the sister can be a good listener to the daughter-in-law's ongoing list of grievances. The sister, though, can be helpful or lead the daughter-in-law astray. For example, if the new bride is unreasonable about what are normal expectations or unrealistic about co-existing with an older relative, the sister that she leans on will push her in one of two directions, especially if the sister has her own heavy load of baggage. The sister can agree with the daughter-in-law's anger and disappointment and nudge her into a warlike path. She might think that support and agreement is really what her sister, the bride, wants, and mistakenly fortify distorted notions, and thus make matters worse. The sibling sister may have her own problem with <u>her</u> own mother-in-law or older women in general and add her own angry agenda to what is initially a natural daughter-in-law discomfort. Then, the mole hill of discomfort turns into a mountain of anger. The sister, sometimes erroneously categorizes the situation as "our family versus theirs", "us against them", and unnecessarily makes matters much worse. Parenthetically, when this sister's supposed support is damaging, she is not moderated as the daughter-in-law is by the fact that this is her loving husband's family after all.

On the flip side, a loving, perceptive sister, especially an older one, can be of great calming assistance to the daughter-in-law. The sister can sometimes review her own history of her relationship with her own husband's mother. She can review what she experienced, some of the mistakes she made, what she learned the hard way, and what she recommends as the wisest path to take. She can assist her in understanding older women, where the latter are coming from and perhaps why the daughter-in-law—mother-in-law syndrome exists in the first place. She can correct faulty logic. She can modify erroneous assumptions. She can help eliminate unrealistic expectations.

Furthermore, she can point out the wonderful aspects of the mother-in-law which are lost in the heat of battle. She can simply point how things could be much worse. She can focus on recognizing the positive and minimizing the negative. She can list the dangers of an ongoing sour mindset between the parties. In addition, she can enumerate the joy of being close with a second set of parents, as well as the long term benefit to the children of this marriage.

All in all, the bride's siblings have a major potential for influencing the mother-in-law—daughter-in-law relationship. Where they are available, sensitive, caring, and wise, they can serve as a wonderful ally to their sister who sits in the "hot seat" and is usually on overload. And those daughters-in-law who have these allies are indeed fortunate.

What of THE SON's siblings, the mother-in-law's other children? Where are they in this hotbed of a scenario? Compared to the siblings of the bride, some things are very much the same and some are understandably different. The major difference is that THE SON'S siblings, again, usually sisters, are giving advice about their mother, not a contemporary! (It is true that indirectly, THE SON's sisters can work on him and he in turn can communicate with both his wife and his mother. However, as stated elsewhere, he plays only a minor role in the conflict of the powerful women who surround him. The reasons? His usual unavailability and his often limited competence in these matters).

On the negative side, a sister can point out to her mother all the failings of the daughter-in-law. Why does she do this? For some of the same reasons that the daughter-in-law's sister might hurtfully interfere. It could be ignorance. It could be misplaced family loyalty. It could be that she perceives of her brother as innocent and gullible, and in need of protection. It might be a conviction that her brother easily could have done much better, and his inexperience and purity made him fair game for his wily choice. The sister might feel that her mother is unraveling emotionally and needs someone to take her side, regardless of the specific issues involved. She might misread her mother's usual wisdom in sizing up people and not see the real factors that are making her mother so upset. She might resent her sister-in-law for taking away her brother, especially if she is very close with him. Lastly, the sister, whether married or single, might be turning into a very jealous woman. She may see her new sister-in-law as taking away the attention she formerly received from her mother, her father, her newly married brother and even any other siblings. She may fear not only losing attention, but gifts, monetary support and communication time as well. Furthermore, if the new daughter-in-law is very pretty or very talented, all the "oohs" and "aahs" that used to be centered around her will now be directed to the newcomer. If her mother, the mother-in-law, is really suffering and not handling things well, she will not help her own daughter through the daughter's rough time as she usually skillfully does. Rather, her mother might grab eagerly for her daughter's faulty support, and the already impossible situation will sadly worsen.

The flip side is the groom's sister helping her mother's anxiety, not by beating up on her new sister-in-law, but by giving wise insightful advice to her mother. She might bring out the special qualities of the daughter-in-law. She might observe how totally happy her brother is since this woman came into his life. She might review the ways that she, the daughter, has been helped by this new member of the family. She might explain to her mother why the daughter-in-law, her own contemporary, acts and speaks as she does in certain situations. She might review with her mother all the problems this inexperienced young woman is coping with, and why survival rather than animosity is foremost on her agenda. She might plea for her mother's patience and tolerance, as difficult as it may seem, as the wisest strategy.

Other relatives like brothers, brothers-in-law and even cousins can play key roles in certain families, depending on the specifics. They too, can alter the chemistry of the classic mother-in-law—daughter-in-law difficulty. Where they are short sighted or have too much of their own agenda clouding their advice, they can be anywhere from mildly harmful to greatly damaging. Where they are gifted with wisdom and awareness, their contributions can be anywhere from comfortably soothing to desperately healing.

# How Was the Mother-In-Law as A Daughter-In-Law?

If a mother-in-law has an instant dislike of her new daughter-in-law, if she wonders how on earth her son, with all the wonderful choices available to him, made this preposterous selection, if she suffers with that which G-d has wrought upon her, and she wails and wails with sadness—does she ever reflect back to her days as a new daughter-in-law? Does she ever think about it? And if she does not, does her former experience play a role in her thought processes whether she likes it or not?

One could postulate that if she had a close, adoring link to her own mother-in-law, then she might have had a built-in subconscious expectation that this would be repeated when it was her turn to be in the role of mother-in-law. If she had such a positive anticipation, would that overrule the reality of what she actually experiences, like a daughter-in-law she deems of low quality, whose house is always messy and who blatantly neglects her children? The answer might be yes. The subconscious programming of an individual can be so strong that it causes strong subjective reactions to different stimuli that the individual is totally unaware of. These reactions can be contrary to the objective facts, and is what we refer to "baggage" or "chemistry" between two people.

On the other hand, twenty years may have passed between a woman as a daughter-in-law and then as a mother-in-law with a lot of water having gone over the dam. There could be no connection at all, with life's vicissitudes cleansing the slate of this subconscious residue.

Supposing our mother-in-law was awful, years ago, as a daughter-in-law. She might have been defensive, snippy, oblivious and openly combative. Will she draw from this experience? Will she remember it at all? Will she consider that after such a bad history, this time around she would make things better? She would remember the waste. She would remember the damage that was inflicted onto the people and children involved. She would, just by sheer determination, orchestrate a happy bond with her son's wife. This kind of mindset would be very positive, and go a long way in overcoming the small irritants that are usually present.

All in all, attitudes and mindsets, whether naturally born or subconscious carryovers from a former time, seem to be major players in the mother-in-law—daughter-in-law combination. They set the expectations. They set the tone. They motivate the desire to do better or they can underly the inclination to be obstructive. They are the directors of this real-life theatre. The actual actors are interchangeable and replaceable. The sets are interesting but just a sideshow. The other minor roles add to the mix but rarely alter the script. The audience awaits the production.

# What About the Grandchildren?

Kids arriving on the scene often improve the relationship between mother-in-law and daughter-in-law. Except in really perverted situations when the kids are used as tools or weapons or miniature messengers between the adversaries, grandchildren bring with them naturally a happy joy to the scene. As in show business when children (and animals) automatically steal any scene in any performance, the mother-in-law—daughter-in-law scene is no different. Unless, of course, the youngsters all look like the daughter-in-law's family which is enough to drive an already distraught mother-in-law over the brink.

For the daughter-in-law, the presence of a mother-in-law, no matter how much the latter is despised, is an instant source of trustable assistance when it comes to the children. When the daughter-in-law has to run over to the doctor with one child who has a frightening fever, she knows that her mother-in-law, where available, will come over to baby sit for the other child in the house. If the daughter-in-law gets a call to pick up her husband at the train station, her previously avoided mother-in-law will get a quick phone call. The daughter-in-law's ability to depend on her, on occasions, usually mini-crisis ones, and the mother-in-law's enjoying the feeling of being needed are very beneficial for the long term connection between the two.

For the mother-in-law, babies and youngsters, regardless of their female source, are bundles of pleasure. She automatically scoops them up with glee whenever she greets them. And the kids feel her warmth and respond accordingly. They give her an instant smile when she walks in the door, and raise their hands expectantly, summoning grandma to lift them up into her arms. The older ones, by conditioning, reflexly ask Grandma at the door, "What did you bring for me, Grandma?" The still older ones are wise enough to check out her hands silently when she visits, correctly feeling secure that somewhere in all those bundles in Grandma's arms, there is a special treat in store for them. The incentive to see the children frequently, watch their development stages, and attend their birthday parties and school plays, serves to pull the mother-in-law to the daughter-in-law's house frequently. Even during the tensest time between the two of them, the daughter-in-law is subconsciously flattered by her mother-in-law's interest in seeing her kids and their growth progress. She is furthermore proud when the kids bring someone, even her mother-in-law, so much glee.

The frequency of these fun visits, as well as the positive responses from the mother-in-law when the daughter-in-law is in trouble, serve to keep the flame glowing, keep up the dialog and to get them accustomed to being in each other's presence. The existence of the children prevents the usual separation that would naturally evolve when two people do not especially like each other. The babies do bring about the geographical closeness that often leads eventually to an emotional closeness.

# Gifts and Invitations are a Form of Dialogue Between the Mother-in-Law and the Daughter-in-Law

When things are not going well between mother-in-law and daughter-in-law, what ensues usually is a separation between the two of them. Separation, amongst all the choices of actions, whether it be short term or long term, is the easiest. Two busy people, even good friends, are often too preoccupied to get together or even to chat. If for not too long a period of time, it is normal and acceptable. It sidesteps the difficult conversation between two people who, at least for the time being, don't like each other. The conversations, when they do occur, run the gamut from stilted to polite to one-word answers to innuendo to double meanings to subtle messages to beating around the bush to talking about the weather and our foreign policy in China. That's when they are civil. When the anger is closer to the surface, the dialogue runs the range of pointed questions and sarcastic answers and accusatory statements, to critical comments, to

<u>no</u> responses, to outright confrontation, and to someone walking out and slamming the door.

Conversations are never easy in these cases. Sometimes they have to be rehearsed beforehand, even in front of a mirror. Sometimes, a list of some kind, whether it be of grievances or requests or arguments to make a point, have to be memorized in advance.

Sometimes, if the grandchildren are old enough, they are unfortunately used as the messengers of the messages between the combatants. "Go, my sweetness, and ask your mother if there are any tissues in this house", or "Go tell you grandmother that her car's wheel is on the grass, and you are afraid the grass underneath might die".

More often, though, the emissary is THE SON himself, the poor soul caught in the middle of these battling giants. "Can you ask your beloved wife why the kids are sitting at the dinner table with hands totally filthy from the playground they just came back from", or "Can you ask my grandson's mother why he is running around the den barefoot. Didn't a glass break in there just this morning?" The politeness is reciprocal. "Will you please ask your mother to change Tommy's socks herself if she thinks they don't match?" Or "Can you please tell your beloved mother that the next time she salts my children's food so much, I'm going to tell her that she's not welcome around here any more." Our poor prince, the son of his angry mother and the husband of his bitter wife, has the awful task of being a world class diplomat to prevent an explosion. And very often, he is not so good at it. Besides, each of these women has a legitimate claim on his siding with her. Often, they are both correct in a particular situation. Sometimes, if he messes up by using the wrong words, he makes things worse. He is always over-tired, hungry and over-extended, to make things worse. However, unlike when the precious little children are used as go-betweens, when <u>he</u> is involved, the stakes are much higher. He is the last hope before outright warfare.

Gifts between the mother-in-law and daughter-in-law are often an unspoken language with very deep meaning. On a simple level, an unusually inexpensive anniversary or birthday gift says "I don't like you, so I'm going to save my money for more worthwhile recipients." A blatantly impersonal gift for an important occasion like a birthday, such as a hedge cutter or bathtub caulking, says "As far as I'm concerned, you are not a real person. If you ever, ever, shape up, I'll take the time to get you something more personal." The gifts, on the other hand, might be, by and large, outright statements of what the recipients might be lacking in the eyes of the donor. The mother-in-law might giver her daughter-in-law a leg shaver or a 20-pack of soap bars or a box of Thank You cards or a fresh pair of slippers or hair conditioner. None of these is innocent, and will successfully fan the flames of a simmering anger. The daughter-in-law might get her mother-in-law a bottle of hair coloring or brown spot remover or an eyeglass chain or a subscription to Modern Maturity. All of these are gunpowder with a pretty ribbon. ("Extreme" gifts are more funny that irritating, such as a bottle of natural herbs to retard memory loss, a case of Depends, a book like "Bringing Up Children for Dummies" or a gift certificate to Doctor Jack Kevorkian.)

Invitations—their timing, their courier and their frequency—are still another form of indirect dialog. A wholesome invitation would be a direct phone call or note between daughter-in-law and mother-in-law, always between the women, who do run the social interactions in most families, to, for example, a holiday dinner. In normal friendly circumstances, the tone of the invite would be upbeat and warm. If it is declined because of scheduling problems or illness of some kind, the one turning it down would sound genuinely disappointed and even suggest an alternate date. Obviously, this gives the one extending herself a good feeling about herself, that her company has value, and that getting together is meaningful and pleasant. The recipient of the overture would likewise be pleased, that the other is pulling her close, that the families really do enjoy each other, and that this process will make for even further togetherness.

When things are not going well, these same invitations, with inappropriate timing, made with an obviously incorrect messenger, or with glaringly pitifully low frequency, are really a hostile act.

Respecting the schedule and concerns of one another is evidenced by an invitation extended at a proper time. Conversely, if a mother-in-law invites her daughter-in-law over for coffee and chat at 6 p.m., the critical hour of feeding, homework and bedtime, her obvious inappropriateness will get her into trouble. The daughter-in-law will get immediately annoyed, and the overture, even if it is sincere, will be totally irritating. Conversely, if the mother-in-law and her husband have a subscription to the opera every Wednesday night for a three month span, a birthday party for the daughter-in-law's one-year old, arranged specifically on a Wednesday night, is an act of war. If the daughter-in-law is nursing an infant every few hours, her mother-in-law's plea to join her on a bus tour of art studios is a request that could never work out at this particular stage and make the daughter-in-law wish she never got the phone call. If the mother-in-law has been in pain for several weeks with a sore hip, she will not be happy if her daughter-in-law invites her to the latter's musical aerobics class. She will correctly consider her daughter-in-law totally dense or an outright wise guy.

Who extends the invitation? Aha! Therein lies the key as to the sincerity or genuineness of the request. As mentioned earlier, the classical donor and recipient are the women of the families, even if the idea was initiated by someone else like a child or a male. If THE SON is an average young adult, he is not comfortable getting involved with planning get-togethers. He is usually in his own world of work, ball-playing, religion, sleep, and more work. Therefore, if HE calls his mother to invite her to have dinner in his house, he had better watch out. His mother will immediately wonder why her daughter-in-law was not making the phone call. She will be certain that her daughter-in-law not only prodded THE SON to make the call, but told him exactly what words to use. And, if the daughter-in-law is angry and is skillful in maneuvering her mate, she, the mother-in-law, might have been told when to come, when to leave, what to bring and what not to bring. The mother-in-law will interpret her daughter-in-law's not getting on the phone as an overt avoidance of having to converse. This is not a particularly subtle message.

Equally bad is having a grandchild call up his grandma, our mother-in-law, and invite her to his own birthday party or "siddur" party. While it normally is cute and touching and pleasantly surprising, it only works well if the two ladies of their respective households are fond of each other. If there is tension or rivalry or hostility or intense dislike, having Junior as the messenger boy will infuriate his grandma. She will feel hurt, perhaps vengeful, and this will often confirm that any hope of a loving closeness is highly improbable.

A mailed invitation is another impersonal act of aggression. Here are two families as closely related as imaginable. To have communication through the U.S. mail, instead of a sweet endearing chat, is an attempt to sabotage the normal closeness expected in loving families.

Likewise, a written note, where a verbal thanks is called for, can also inflame the combatants. If one has gone out of the way for the other or has been unusually generous, a loving appreciative acknowledgement would be the norm. A lukewarm thank you card would always be a deep disappointment and only serve to confirm that there has been no progress towards a real thaw.

How frequently do the invitations come between the daughter-in-law's and mother-in-law's families? Right here is the barometer of how the relationship is going. When you like people, you cannot wait to see them and look for every opportunity to spend time together. Everyone makes choices. Both the mother-in-law and daughter-in-law have friends and relatives not related to the other. There are many scheduling opportunities customarily available for visits. Ordinary weekends, holidays, birthday celebrations and graduations constantly come up. When things are not going well, the daughter-in-law will be spending lots of time at <u>her</u> mother's house and chatting with <u>her</u> endlessly on the phone. Or, she will be hanging out in the house of one of her siblings. As it is, her husband's extended family is new and somewhat foreign to her. It does not take much, especially in these difficult newlywed years, to stay far away.

Likewise, the older mother-in-law over the years has set up comfortable social patterns. She is very comfortable in her daughter's home. After all, for the most part, it is similar in style to her own home. She has developed many friendships over the years, accumulated at different ages and different places, and she cherishes the company of her favorites. She has learned through life experience how to foster the warmth of the associations that make her feel good. Likewise, she has the wisdom as to how to tactfully avoid the uncomfortable connections. If she dislikes her daughter-in-law and still has not recovered from her son's questionable choice, she will avoid their getting together and keep the interaction at a diplomatic minimum. Of course, by minimizing the offering and accepting of invitations involving her daughter-in-law, she cuts down on the pleasures of the company of her delightful son and her son's children.

All in all, the logistics and means of communication and frequencies of invitations between mother-in-law and daughter-in-law will pattern themselves after the quality and status of the relationship between the parties. Not only will they serve as an indicator of the status quo, but they will be used as the ongoing indirect language between these ladies. When things are gloomy, they will serve as painful weapons. When the atmosphere is chummy and comfortable, they will be vehicles for further togetherness.

# Sons-in-Law

Why don't mother-in-laws have as many problems with their sons-in-law and why is there not the classic son-in-law—mother-in-law battle which corresponds to that of the daughter-in-law—mother-in-law? Actually, in some situations, there is sad hostility between the two, causing great grief in the families. But usually, there is not the classic standoff. The biggest reason is that men are so different than women emotionally.

Men for the most part live in a world of work and play. Young marrieds, most having a living mother-in-law, are working under tension at one, two or three jobs to make ends meet for their family, and even eke out a contribution to the family nest egg. Men's <u>identity</u> is often their work, their skill, their profession. If you posed the question to men and women to describe who they are, the women would initially identify themselves as wives or mothers. Further down the list, they would add a profession or skill or a degree that they possess.  Men usually identify themselves by their work, how they make a living.  They may be great fathers to their children, doting sons to their parents, and attentive husbands, but their title is usually their working title.

Men's other main focus is usually physical fitness in some form.  They are born with masculine energy and sexuality and aggression.  The aggression portion of their hormones, if they are clean living and honest, shows up as competitiveness in a sport.  Their rage and hostility is permissible in a game.  The competition may be landing an illusive tuna on a deep sea fishing trip.  The competition could be a whole team as in basketball.  It could be against one person as in squash or tennis. It could be against themselves when they jog against the clock or hit a bucket of balls on a golf range.  (Years ago, I used to humorously prod my children into increased competitiveness while participating in a sport. "If you have to crash into a wall to reach a ball during a game, do it!  An injured shoulder or wrist will eventually heal, but a lost point is a point lost forever.")

In terms of relationships, men are again very different from their female counterparts. Girls grow up as social beings.  One of their highest priorities from the beginning is their relationship with other girls.  Their days are often rated by how they feel about their friends and vice versa.  "I met a very nice girl in school who just transferred from another school."  or "I am furious.  My best friend just gave me the cold shoulder." or "I was looking everywhere for Mindy and when I found her, there she was, whispering with a girl I can't stand."  Even more than her hair, this is what makes her world turn.  Their buddies, their rivals, their former friends, the leaders of the pack, girls they secretly admire—all are private obsessions that go on during their school day and family time. This long time focus on relationships, furthermore, is the reason why, in many cases, women go into marriage far more prepared for the upcoming partnership than their new husbands. The women have the sensitivity background and more advanced communications skills than the men they marry because this has been their focus all along.

Men's relationships with other men very commonly are "activity" relationships. "I'd like you to meet Gregg, my golfing buddy." or, "I'll be a little late tonight, honey. A few of the guys are going to stop off for a beer on the way home from the meeting."

Male friends usually <u>do</u> things together. They may talk about sports or women or the stock market, but it's usually while putting on their sneakers together, or briefly in the sauna after a game. Their interest in each other is primarily for the game, and often is not there before or after. Personal feelings or concerns are not the usual fare for subject matter. So, in fact, they often do not really know each other well. After ten years of playing racquetball, if asked how many children his long time opponent had, he'd probably hesitate for a minute and then say, "Oh I don't know. A bunch, I think." If asked where he lived, the response might be, "Uh, I think about 15 minutes from the court." (In a weekly basketball game over a twenty-year span, the same ten to fifteen players came down Thursday after Thursday. A particular fellow who had not come down for a month had sustained an Achilles heal injury and was in a cast. One day, somebody happened to think of him and dialed his number just to see how he was feeling. He said that the recovery period was a slow process, but that his pain had almost gone and that he was feeling well. Before he hung up, he commented casually that after a month of absence from the Thursday night game, this was the first call he had received from any participant in the game. Generalizations are risky, but this is fairly typical of the type of connection that men make with each other.)

A son-in-law is not particularly connected emotionally with his mother-in-law. Unless they hit it off from the start with great chemistry, or he goes into marriage looking for a replacement for a mother that he once had or wished he had, their connection is not usually a deep one. He enjoys the high status in his in-laws' eyes because he did indeed finally marry their single daughter and take her off their hands. He is connected to his mother-in-law because she does cheerfully run over to babysit for their infant child when something comes up at the last minute. He does enjoy his wife's closeness with his mother, a real friendship with lots of sharing—unless, of course, it is unnaturally close and it interferes with his marriage. In general, he is treated very well by his mother-in-law. When he and his wife, the daughter, visit the mother-in-law, the daughter is treated as a daughter who slides right back into her adolescent role. He is initially treated politely as a guest and eventually, if things go well, he slides over more and more in the direction of being a son. The mother-in-law does not have a pivotal role in the son-in-law's psyche. He works. She runs her own home.

There are no areas for comparison or competition, as there is with a daughter-in-law who also runs a home. He is usually not around. He doesn't get especially involved in common family misunderstandings and feuds.

To be on his mother-in-law's good list, all he has to do is satisfactorily take care of her expected list of obligations, and he need score no higher mark than a C to pass muster. He must take care of his wife, the mother-in-law's daughter, to the extent that she goes around looking happy and functioning well. He must support his new family financially in a dependable responsible way. He is expected to bring up the grandchildren in a kind, supportive manner. He must help with the physical running of the house. He should be the spiritual leader of his family and set an example of good deeds and ethical behavior.

To his mother-in-law, he is like a combination guest and relative. The connection is intellectual rather that emotional. It is casual and peripheral rather than intensely central. Unlike the daughter-in-law where every word, opinion, reaction, tone, gesture, theory, recipe, decision and response is under intensely judgmental scrutiny and evaluation, he gets a relatively free ride.

To further please his mother-in-law and keep their connection a peaceful one, he must avoid pitfalls that might drive her batty. Any nonsense theories of parenting or questionable fiscal strategies or irritating habits that he brought with him as baggage from his nuclear family must be kept quiet or, at least, understated. Any irritating personality flaws or manner of speaking must be instantly corrected by a wise wife who can admonish him softly in his ear. He must learn when to "fake it" and other forms of civility when around a mother-in-law that he doesn't know so well yet. Any food she works hard on to please him should always get a compliment even if the taste is foreign to what he is accustomed to. He <u>must</u> help make decisions on critical family choices even if he has absolutely no interest or experience in these areas. For example, "Which of the interior decorator's choices of window treatment does he think would look best in this room?" "Which of these dresses should I keep, honey, and which should I return?" "What color scheme for the next wedding would look best in this particular catering hall?" He must try to remember important anniversary dates and birthdays. It comes with the turf.

He does have one sensitive area concerning his mother-in-law which can convert this polite relationship into a tense volatile one. It has to do with how his wife gets along with her mother. As per the old adage that when your kids marry, you keep your daughters and you lose your sons. In most cases, the daughter, trained in domesticity by her mother, will perpetuate the latter's content and style. The daughter so steeped in her mother's decorating, cooking, values, scheduling, and priorities, except in the particular areas that she has a problem with, will repeat the "wife and mother" methods of her mom.

Certain problems do come up with mother and daughter, and will interfere with the peace and happiness of the son-in-law and his wife.

Firstly, the mother-in-law as the mother of her own daughter, may have a criticizing, demeaning, deprecatory style when it comes to the way her daughter does things. She may constantly put her down, driving her into a low self-esteem as a wife and mother. As a result, the daughter may frequently return from these conversations or sessions feeling depressed, helpless, and inept. When this is the state of mind with which she greets her husband, the son-in-law, after a long tiring day at work, he is going to be correctly resentful. If this scenario is ongoing, he will become a mean, protective antagonist to his mother-in-law. Either there will be uncomfortable confrontations at the slightest hint of his wife's being upset by her mother, or the reverse will happen. Not comfortable with not only the damage he perceives his wife is receiving, or the angry vengeful person he himself has become, he will opt for separation. He will seek to separate himself, his wife, and any children from this threat to his tranquil domesticity.

For survival, the formerly passive son-in-law will become the aggressive protector of his brood.

Secondly, another common mother-daughter relationship may equally threaten the son in law's peace. The mother and daughter might be too close. His wife, he realizes belatedly, may never have properly separated from her mom. The mother might love the connection, having her cake and eating it, i.e. getting her daughter married off and yet keeping her dependent. The daughter, in extreme situations, might call her mother up for decision making and opinions ten times a day for ten different issues. The daughter might confide in her mother on personal items rather than the normal confiding in her own husband. She might review her day, her relationships, her anxieties and her plans with her mom, and have little to share with her husband when he returns from work. He will gradually absorb that his wife is not maturing as an adult, and their closeness as a married couple is just not happening. He will constantly accuse her of being married to her mother. He will take out his unhappiness on his mother-in-law. Faulting the older of the two, who should know better, this "guest-relative" of a son-in-law will become a spiteful adversary. And again, when he can change his family's location to break the umbilical cord, he will. When he cannot separate geographically, he will use every strategy to separate the families and reduce the frequency of their get-togethers.

In general, though, the mother-in-law will consider her connection with her son-in-law a piece of cake as compared to that with her daughter-in-law. The son-in-law will just be there, while her daughter-in-law, by definition, doing the same irritating things as her son-in-law, will drive her nuts.

# The Role of the Father-in-Law

The father-in-law in this crisis will deal with the problem from a much different vantage point than his wife. He will be very connected to the goings on, but from his own perspective. What is he occupied with? For one, he is likewise upset by his son's selection of a mate, but the disappointment is more of an intellectual one rather than an emotional one. Secondly, he is faced with his own beloved wife being out of control, something he is definitely not accustomed to. Thirdly, he is very much involved with wedding arrangements and its associated expenses which is a problematic reality he has to deal with. Lastly, not by his own choice, he is thrown into a new relationship—with the bride's parents. It is with the latter that he becomes a new business partner in a huge financial expenditure, the wedding. He also becomes a partner in the procedural selections of the wedding ceremony. He is also a future partner of financial assistance toward the setting up of the newlywed apartment, as well as possibly the expected babysitting scheduling further up the road.

The father-in-law, very closely connected to his son, was always in a bind during his son's dating period. Deep down, he assumed that his son, if he were generally happy with his upbringing and the atmosphere of his home, would probably select a wife type that would somewhat duplicate a household and marriage pattern similar to his own. For example, if the relationship of his parents was a romantic one, then he would expect his son to seek out a girl that would bring out romantic attention from him. If his father had a lukewarm attachment to his mother and they both worked hard at their respective job with long hours, then his son might follow accordingly. If there was a battling or argumentative style of communication in the home, then his boy would probably not be attracted to someone with a "mashed potatoes" personality. (Or, the equally common scenario of a son rebelling against what was an uncomfortable air in his home, and deliberately seeking to change it!)

The father-in-law invariably will be disappointed in his new daughter-in-law. Without necessarily realizing it, his disapproval might be primarily due solely to the newness of this added family member. For starters, he may not find her attractive as a woman and wonder what his son sees in her. Her voice is different than his wife and daughters. She has different ideas, a different temperament, a different sensitivity level, and a different pace of doing things. She responds differently, she eats differently, she dresses differently and she moves differently.

He has no anticipated deep investment in his relationship with her. As a man, his relationships in general are not as deep as his female counterparts. He is very close to his wife and daughters, and their reaction to the newcomer does impact him. He loves his son very much and does want him to be happy. However, when a son marries, as opposed to a daughter, the son is often "lost" from his original family. The son now belongs to a stranger, and the house she sets up is in her style and taste, which is, after all, foreign to her father-in-law. Since it is the daughter-in-law who runs the home, when he visits, the father-in-law will always initially feel somewhat detached as he would when he visits a neighbor to borrow a quart of milk. Depending on the dynamics of the relationship with this newcomer as well as the frequency of his visits to her home, usually this awkward barrier will, for the most part, dissipate. The father-in-law will be visiting his future grandchildren and there will be regular family get-togethers, so a thaw in the relationship's initial chill can be expected. (The father-in-law usually does not go through this detached initiation period when his own daughter marries. Most daughters set up house like their mothers. Except where they rebel or move far away, they cook like their mothers and run a family pattern like their mothers. Their father, entering their homes when they are first married, will generally find it a cozy and familiar experience, even though their husbands are new to him, and he will adapt quicker to the new situation.)

Since men's preoccupations are usually with their work and play, the impact of the new daughter-in-law in the family on him will be less profound than on his wife. In time, he will become more and more comfortable in his relationship with his daughter-in-law as the rough spots smooth out. In a minority of cases, they will become very close and have a very loving father-daughter kinship. In the majority of cases, though, the relationship will be friendly and cordial but not notably deep. The father-in-law will be primarily interested in the affairs of his son as an extension of himself. He will likewise be submerged in a loving supportive chemistry with his son's children. He will have great pride in this fledgling family. Blood is thicker than water. Exceptions are always around. In most cases, the daughter-in-law will always be the slightly distanced administrator of the father-in-law's very close attachment to his son and his son's children.

Where emotion is very strong for the father-in-law is what is going on with his wife and daughters during the entrée of the daughter-in-law into the family situation. When his wife is upset, the father-in-law is no longer a lukewarm observer on the scene. When his wife is irrationally unhappy, which is unusual for him to see, nothing is right anywhere, and he will have no peace in his life. The father-in-law will turn into a protective lion, and rush to seek solutions to the specific problem areas. If the anxiety comes from the financial negotiations with his future daughter-in-law's parents, he will find himself surprisingly aggressive in his dealings with them. He will not exhibit the patience and desire to please as he would with his customers at his own work place. If the future daughter-in-law is disrespectful in action or words to his wife, his reaction will be rapid and harsh to her or to his son, even probably an overreaction. If the father-in-law's own daughters are upset with their brother's selection of a wife or they see things that are bad omens for their brother's future, their father will take on their battle cry. If later on, the daughter-in-law's parenting techniques drive his female blood relatives into a frenzy, the protective father-in-law, usually the relaxed silent diplomat on the scene, will find his tongue considerably loosened. He will be rough. He will interfere. He will trespass. He will be surprisingly pushy. He will only relax when his wife and daughters can relax, and hopefully, the damage that he causes will not be too hurtful and will ultimately be forgotten.

In summary, the father-in-law's role in the arrival of the daughter-in-law on the scene is not a particularly profound one. He has two potentially sensitive areas invested in this time period. Firstly, if he thinks the world of his son, consciously or subconsciously, justifiably or unjustifiably, he thinks that his son could have done a lot better in his selection of a lifetime partner. This feeling sits not too deeply from the surface. Therefore, any conflict or irritation caused by the bride or her parents or her siblings or her friends will cause an eruption in this usually tolerant man. He will immediately want to swoop up his son into his protective arms and press the eject button to rid his life and his son's life of the undeserving intruder. All his outward actions will come from his basically disapproving anger, which in most cases, fortunately, will never be acted on.

Secondly, anyone or anything that upsets his wife, whether it be a plumber or a butcher or a neighbor, throws him into an irrational state of mind, capable of projecting him into the worst primitive behavior. All his civility and logic and tolerance immediately goes out the window. He becomes a vengeful child. He knows that this demon is within him and must always be restrained. As a matter of fact, by now, his wife and probably his son know his boiling point and probably are wise enough to hide from him most of the inflammatory goings on. But the demon does lurk beneath.

Demons aside, the prognosis for the father-in-law—daughter-in-law bonding is good to excellent. In time, children, holidays, family get-togethers, and good food will wear down the rough spots. The good will prevail over the bad. As the mother-in-law gradually does better, her mate will do better by her side. Not to be overlooked, the father-in-law, as the less emotional in-law, will be an excellent constructive ingredient in the family dynamics. His logic, his wise overview, his love of peace will be a terrific influence on the more emotional ladies in his life, and he will be a great asset to family unity.

# __Humor__

Is there any place for humor to help alleviate some of the pain and tension between mother-in-law and daughter-in-law? The answer is a resounding "NO".

Wait! Before humor is discarded quickly, let it be qualified that any humor will <u>not</u> be between the two combatants. When it comes to relationships, women, by their built-in nature, do not see anything funny about things. They are emotional creatures. They have a lot vested here. There is deep anxiety. There is great disappointment on both sides. The issues are not superficial. They are real and they are deep and they will not go away. In the presence of pain, there is no room for frivolity.

However, men are created of a different material. With some exceptions, their relationships do not go as deep as their female counterparts. They are able to step outside of situations, even those they are very much involved in, and look for humor or distraction to deal with tension.

A fun-loving father-in-law can go a long way toward relieving the unhappiness of his wife as well as bringing out a smile on the face of his daughter-in-law. If he is good at it, where he is aware but not obsessed, teasing but not confrontational, somewhat intolerant but not overly judgmental—then, he can be very helpful to make things better. Example:

The mother-in-law and father-in-law visit their daughter-in-law's apartment. With smiles and greetings, they cross the living room into the kitchen. The mother-in-law is immediately ready to collapse at the 30-second mark of her visit. (That's because she used up 20 seconds to remove her coat!) There is the familiar smell of a bowel movement diaper on, or rather half on fifteen-month old Andrew, who unsteadily walks across the room to greet them. He has a welt on his forehead from the previous day's fall onto the edge of the cocktail table. He is wearing one sock with no shoes. In his right hand is an onion roll as big as his head with one mini-bite bitten out of it. His left hand is sticky from something that looks like chocolate pudding (at least we hope it's chocolate pudding), holding his mommy's car keys with a big smile on his face. There are toy pieces, none matching, all over the floor. His "sippy cup" is lying on its side, open, in a pool of apple juice. The Venetian blinds on the large window are tipped on an angle with one of the upper attachments off its hook. There is folded up underwear, recently laundered, strewn everywhere over the floor coming from a pile that mommy had probably been folding before she was distracted, courtesy of Andrew. There is white powder on the floor everywhere, maybe flour, maybe talcum powder, with footprints of a toddler trailing off in every direction. Mommy, after having answered the door, is in the kitchen on the phone, holding a coffee mug, chatting with a smile on her face. She is wearing a bathrobe, frayed along the sleeves and bottom hem, covering a not-matching pajama top and bottom. It's 1 p.m. in the afternoon. It is true that this particular visit was unannounced, with mother-in-law and father-in-law in the neighborhood shopping, and deciding to stop by at the last minute.

While the mother-in-law is fit to be tied, her husband thinks this scene is hysterically funny. He could not imagine the best stage director having enough imagination and ingenuity to set this up for a scene in a theatre. With sticky flour and crunchy Cheerios under his shoes, his steps make a funny sound. Sound effects! When his daughter-in-law finally finishes talking to her friend, he rushes up to her mimicking a panic look on his fact. "Are you all alright, Charlotte? It looks like there was an awful explosion here. Is everyone okay? On, my gosh, look at all the damage! You must be so frightened. And Andrew! Was he injured by the impact? Look at all the mess it made!"

The beleaguered daughter-in-law forces a smile. "Very cute, Dad. Very clever."

She is mostly focusing on her mother-in-law who looks as pale as a ghost. Her father-in-law, she perceives, is just a funny lightweight by comparison. In this embarrassing moment, she cannot help but laugh. He did, as usual, defuse the tension. "Why didn't you call first and tell me you were coming?" She asks. "I was folding some laundry when my friend phoned in a panic over a problem she was having. Why don't you both come in and sit in the kitchen. I'll have this room cleaned up in a second."

The father-in-law and mother-in-law enter the kitchen. What strikes their eyes first is the massive high pile, in both sinks, of dirty dishes, pots, and silverware. It looked like a whole week's accumulation, although in actuality it was from a party they had given for neighborhood friends the day before. The mother-in-law swallows hard and hides her eyes from the mess. She collapses into a chair and looks out the window. Her pitiful gaze seems to be upward in the neighborhood of G-d. Her husband could not resist. "Charlotte, come in here! I want you to see something amazing." She shuffles into the kitchen in her slippers with a hole in front of each of her big toes. "You must see this", he says excitedly. "You know, I have never seen anything like this before. Look at your sinks. You must have broken the Guinness Book of Records with those piles. Amazing! Can I run out to the car and get my Polaroid camera? This must be documented for posterity. Maybe we could bronze the piles and keep them as an exhibit!"

Charlotte, the daughter-in-law, smiles through a big yawn, that is, a 1 p.m. yawn. "We got finished with last night's party very late, Dad, and we both collapsed as soon as the last guest left. Don't worry, I'll take care of it." She looks at the piles. She giggles. "Dad," she says, "I don't know why, but you always make me laugh."

The father in law, feeling totally relaxed, eases into a dining room chair. He looks around casually and suddenly realizes something he never noticed before in his son's apartment. All ten of the chairs around the dining room table are different. A couple are formal chairs, loosened up at their joints, remnants of an old dining room set. A couple are light wood chairs borrowed from a kitchen set. There is one stool. A few non-matching folding chairs round out the lot. For a family married almost eight years, this seemed a little odd, considering that the dining room is often the social get together room, and expanding one's friends is usually a high priority. Simply stated, a good dining set is often one of the first pieces of furniture purchased by a young family.

"Charlotte", he calls out, trying to figure out how to get his gently intolerant message across without doing too much harm, "Charlotte, look at how giving a person you are. You keep ten different chairs around your dining room table to please ten different tastes. Ten different guests can find their own special preference in chair styles. You are such a good soul."

Looking for a cold drink, the suffering mother-in-law's husband pokes through the refrigerator. He can be heard chuckling. Another museum piece here, he thinks, scanning the shelves. A dirty pot with no cover, holding about a tablespoon of yesterday's food takes up most of the tall shelf. Two pears, each with two bites missing, fall to the floor. Plastic containers containing miscellaneous leftovers adorn the shelves. Some have covers. Some don't. Some have covers that fall into the container. Some have the wrong size cover. Something red and sticky coats all the shelves on the right side. Probably, something fell over on the top shelf and leaked down all the way to the bottom. He picks up the mushy pears and is at a loss where to put them. The scene seems like a caricature of a refrigerator's contents, compared to the real clean look that his wife maintains in their own kitchen. He imagines Norman Rockwell transfixed by the special look here and using it as a painting for the cover of an issue of Saturday Evening Post. He opens the freezer looking for ice. Startled, he immediately slams the freezer door shut. It was crammed with pots, packages, and uncovered food—all tipped to the front ready to fall out. If they did fall out, it would be like a glacier wall sheering off its surface. One had better be wearing iron-tipped shoes, and one had better have a least two days available to clean up the bloody mess. "Charlotte", he calls out. "Charlotte, come in here! You must see this. I have some exciting news for you! I'm here in the kitchen." Resigned, she shuffles up to his side, part of her bathrobe's hem trailing after her. "What is it, Dad?" "Guess what, Charlotte. You have another child! I opened the freezer door and he is hiding in there behind a pot. Andrew has a brother. This calls for a celebration. Why don't you take a look? Mazel Tov!" She squeezes out a smile. His sense of humor is starting to get to her. She knows intellectually that he is openly critical of just about everything. However, she instinctively analyzes that if he can get it all out in jest, it cannot really bother him that much. And therefore, he really likes her. She takes this as a compliment, despite the content of his underlying message. She breaks into a laugh.

The father-in-law takes his wife home. That was a fun visit for him. She is quiet.

# There Are Some Great Mother-in-Law—Daughter-in-Law Relationships

Although there is great evidence that mothers-in-law and daughters-in-law do not do well without lots of effort by both parties, there are many exceptions to the rule. This latter group would question the whole premise of this book. Yes, there are daughters-in-law and mothers-in-law who love each other like daughter and mother, and even consider this attachment the closest one that they have in their lives. There is warmth. They stay in constant touch. They share feelings. They root for one another. They look for every opportunity to get together. They look for every means of making the other feel good—whether it be in words or acts or gifts.

Why do these special attachments exist? As in other relationships, there are many reasons, reasons that arise from one of the two parties involved or both.

From the daughter-in-law's vantage point one reason might be pure chemistry. In the package together with a new husband arrives this woman who magically is instantly special. It could be her appearance, the way she talks, her personality, her style of doing things, her way of seeing things or even just how she focuses on her, the daughter-in-law. Since the beginning of time, chemistry between two beings, whether they be robins or frogs or camels or new relatives is a very real phenomenon. It is very legitimate and valid and part of life.

Another reason that a daughter-in-law might be attached to her new mother-in-law is that the latter is a replacement for the mother that she never had, or used to have, or wished she had. Her mother-in-law is a substitute who fills her need to be nurtured or to whom to give nurture. She fills the void. Unless the mother-in-law blows the opportunity by being oblivious of this fortuitous situation or too extreme in this or that to be easily lovable, she has an advantage from day one that many of her contemporaries don't enjoy.

Another scenario might occur when the daughter-in-law is bowled over or at least highly flattered by an arriving mother-in-law who is crazy about her. The daughter-in-law might have her own initial reservations about this older woman. However, everyone loves to be loved, and in turn finds herself loving the person who loves her. So the daughter-in-law is more or less won over by the positive attention her new mother-in-law showers on her, even though the daughter-in-law did not experience a particularly positive feeling from the start.

Some daughters-in-law are, by nature, individuals who attach easily. They feel good inside their own skin. They are happy. They are content. They like just about everyone around them unless they are particularly offensive. They see the good in people. So, together with a new husband that she adores, arrives his mother. Simply by extension, she greets and accepts this older woman as a new part of her life, someone who will be an automatic part of her now expanded family. Her mother-in-law is merely someone additional on her long list of people to love, and she bonds quickly with the new arrival.

The mother-in-law, from her own perspective, can experience similar good feelings. She, too, may experience instant chemistry with her new daughter-in-law. Regardless of their generation gap differences, regardless of their extremely different ways of doing things, there is a strong attraction. They rapidly become good close friends and enjoy each other immensely.

Likewise, her new daughter-in-law might be a substitute for a daughter that she never had and wished she had. She immediately attaches herself to her son's wife and treats her like her own flesh and blood. The mother-in-law might have literally no daughters of her own or have a difficult relationship with them that pain her endlessly. She may have daughters who live far away, who followed their husband's jobs, and she may not have the joy of day to day communication or seeing her grandchildren develop. She may suffer from this longing. Her new daughter-in-law, if she lives nearby, gives her a reprieve, a new daughter to start over with, and to share life with.

Mirroring the daughter-in-law's reasons for experiencing a loving bonding with her mother-in-law, a mother-in-law might be overwhelmed by the warmth that her new daughter-in-law bestows upon her. The older woman, despite seeing all the flaws in her son's selection for a wife, is flattered and overcome by the love toward her exhibited by her new daughter-in-law. Her daughter-in-law thinks she is fantastic. Her daughter-in-law solicits her advice, offers her help constantly, and looks for every chance to get together. Her daughter-in-law thinks that not only did she marry the best guy in the world, but his mom is a superwoman. Well, very few mothers-in-law can resist this attention, and their positive responses lead to a lifelong bonding.

Some mother-in-laws are cheery, happy individuals who feel joy and appreciation of what life has offered them. They like people. They have upbeat attitudes. A new daughter-in-law in the family? Well, you can bet your bippy that she is going to take this young inexperienced little girl under her wing and shower her with love, emotional support, and encouragement. So what if these babies have shortcomings or distorted ideas from their nuclear families. They will be smothered with caring warmth. They need the protective guidance of an older guardian.

Finally, some mother-in-laws simply have a rational and logical way of looking at situations. They love their sons. They are thrilled that their boys put aside their books and their work, and put in the effort to find the right girl to marry. They are thrilled that their sons are settling down and will indeed be family men. These mothers-in-law want to do what is right and what is expected of them. It is very obvious to them that they want to rapidly welcome the new bride into their arms and their homes. They want to help these fledgling wives with decorating, shopping advice and, eventually, babysitting. They want to give them the benefit of their years of experience. They want to assist these young women to be successful homemakers for their sons. They want their sons to stay close, and be proud of their mom's support.

As we can see, there are many underlying reasons for the great mother-in-law—daughter-in-law relationships that do exist. In some cases, the close attachment will be pre-programmed from an inner need or expectation or obligation. In other cases, the relationship starts out tentatively, but the positive steps taken by one of the parties draws the other one into the fold. It really makes no difference. What counts is the result. This group of mothers-in-law and daughters-in-law who can experience close, adoring attachments are very blessed. Warmth begets warmth.

Their bonding can set up an extended family of children and parents and grandparents who can all benefit from this well of nurture and comfort for years and years. How fortunate they are.

# General Recommendations

Because of the huge variety of scenarios leading up to the mother-in-law—daughter-in-law relationship, it must be understood that a list of educated suggestions will never apply completely in one family. People are so different. Their in-coming baggage is so varied. Finances, location, extended family, previous marriages, religion, presence of children, work pressures, physical handicaps, peer pressures, housing setup, available outside resources and individual dispositions, are just a few of the factors that make for astronomic variations in any family situation. It is impossible to judge someone else's functioning without being in their shoes. The objective facts may be there to see, but feelings and emotions and what goes on in someone's heart are only known to that person alone.

However, repeated human behavioral patterns, life experience, general logic and eternal hope combine to create the following list of recommendations. If only one of the several on the list make just one individual just a mite happier, even for a fleeting moment, the brave attempt is worth it.

(1) Number one on the list is for every married couple to work as hard as they can to have the best marriage possible. Hopefully, with children involved, not only will they be visible daily role models, but they will be able to actively teach these children about the skills necessary for <u>their</u> future unions. The married couple must convey the importance of a well functioning marriage because their children will frequently follow in their footsteps and their children in their footsteps and so on. Therefore, every individual on this ladder has the burden of the next few generations on his or her shoulders. They are not working in a vacuum. Just as parents are painfully exacting in their toilet training techniques and teaching their youngsters how to read, they must work on building character and teaching relationship skills early in life. And when their kids are dating and at the age when they would prefer to share confidential thoughts with their contemporaries, their parents cannot be passive observers. They must be involved, listening, making adjustments on faulty notions, and pressing for healthy attitudes and values. If they cannot be there at this critical age, because of work schedule pressure or health limitations, someone old and wise has to be the surrogate teacher. Girls, in particular, must not only be educated as to what guys are made of, but of supreme importance, they should never lose track of the highest healthy priority for themselves: marriage, home and children.

(2) Pre-marital courses and counseling in schools as a required curriculum is still in its infancy. Its critical importance must be recognized. Two young kids cannot select a mate just because the other one is cute. Functioning once married is by far too complex for on-the-job training. A young man cannot get on the tennis court for the first time and be ready to compete in a tournament. He must learn form and strokes. He must read tennis books. He must take lessons from an expert. After that, it is endless practice and study until he is anywhere near ready. Dating kids must know their obligations as marriage partners in advance. They must know which expectations are realistic and which are not. They must learn communication skills. They must have at least some basic parenting skills. They must be exposed to the scheduling problems of juggling work, recreation, parenting, and togetherness time in a busy week. They must learn the business side of family choices—which charities, how much, recreation budgets, housekeeping expenses, baby sitting costs, choices of schools, choices of neighborhoods to live in, pre-nuptial agreements, and so on. Like learning to be a doctor or lawyer, they must recognize that being married is a separate complicated world different from anything they experienced earlier. Naturally, this huge training must be upbeat and totally optimistic. Failure—separation or divorce—must be presented as <u>not</u> being an option, except in unusual extreme cases. Marriage must be depicted as a wonderful state to be in. Having a lifetime pal of one's very own to share endless years with is the ultimate prize. Furthermore, a country made up of traditional families, two parents and children living together in one

household, is a country most apt to possess a high ethical fabric of behavior and a low level of drugs and crime.

(3) Young newlyweds should initially live at a distance from both sets of parents. This may seem contradictory to the idealized scenario of the young couple living in the same house or on the same street as one set of parents. The parents help with the cooking, the decorating of the trainee apartment, the financing, and the decision making. Eventually, the parents are there for babysitting, medical emergencies, and dealing with tough repairmen. The rosy picture continues with their attending religious services together and making holiday celebrations bigger, warmer, busier and friendlier. All of this is, arguably, great two years up the road, but injurious to the marriage immediately after the wedding. It is imperative, unless there are major health or financial problems, for the new bride and groom to be off on their own. Only by separating from close relatives and lifelong friends can they really get to know one another. They can learn to problem solve together. They can lean on each other rather than look elsewhere for help during difficult times. They can explore each other's minds and hopes and dreams and worries and regrets. They can share the special delight of learning new things together, exploring new places, new ideas, new hobbies and any new experiences. Because they are alone, this intimate friendship growth is not diluted with the intrusion of even very well meaning constant visitors. In their young inexperienced lives, they have a close partner to share the maturing process. They get to be really solid good

friends. Their marriage will not be a casual, doing-the-expected-correct-thing relationship.

When this internship is over, however long as it takes, they can rejoin their old friends and waiting relatives. However, they return as a tight family unit, much better qualified to deal with life's complexities than if they had omitted this vital private maturing period.

For the young bride, now emotionally more stabilized, her relationships with her mother-in-law and her other new and old relatives have a much improved prognosis. More secure within her own skin, more loved then she had ever experienced before, and with a best friend, she can look forward in every way to getting closer with her mother-in-law. She is less apt to overreact, to lose her temper, to take revenge on her husband. She is simply better qualified to make the best of her relationship with her mother-in-law and the others who surround her.

(4) Where possible, the mother-in-law and daughter-in-law should avoid words and acts that are irreversible and cause a deep scar hampering any future attempts for closeness. Certain statements will never be forgotten and can never be taken back. If the mother-in-law says things with a definite intent to hurt, she will hit a nerve with subsequent permanent damage. For example, if the mother-in-law alludes to any deficiency in the daughter-in-law's mother, she is usually in big trouble. Even if the daughter-in-law actually dislikes her own mother, hearing something negative from the mouth of her mother-in-law will elicit from her a protective rage. If the mother-in-

law alludes to some alleged secret in the daughter-in-law's family, such as someone having spent time in prison or a family business having gone bankrupt or some illegitimate baby being born, she is "cruising for a bruising". On the flip side, certain words exploding from a bitter daughter-in-law about her mother-in-law will become a lifelong wound, guaranteed. If she calls her mother-in-law "a senile wacko" or someone who "dresses like a harlot" or someone who is a "bad seed who ruined her whole family including the son I'm married to", she is on the hit list forever. If either scream that the other is never welcome in her home again, that might be taken literally for the foreseeable future. If the mother-in-law allegedly poisons her grandchildren's minds about how bad their mother is, or if the daughter-in-law viciously exposes her husband's irregularities to his all loving mother, it would take years and years for these words to be forgotten and forgiven.

Prevention is the only way of dealing with hurtful outbursts between mother-in-law and daughter-in-law. As pertains to any relationship, the parties must mature emotionally to the extent that irrevocable slips of the tongue will never happen.

(5) Patience, considerable patience, is a virtue desperately needed for anything new in life.

(6) Prayer. Lots of prayer.

# The Ultimate Responsibility Rests on the Mother-in-Law

When the unstoppable force meets the immovable object, something has to give. If the mother-in-law and daughter-in-law are at war, and each of their list of grievances is absolutely correct, what will be? If each is stuck in the mud and cannot proceed, then what? If each acts totally inappropriately at every opportunity and prevents any glimmer of a reconciliation, what can we hope for? If both slide into a state of war, get pretty comfortable with that state, and are more than content to stay there, then what? While every situation is totally different from the next, and every warring party is a bundle of numerous complexities, the premise that is proposed here is that it is the responsibility of improvement rests with the mother-in-law.

Why? Because the mother-in-law, usually at least twenty years her daughter-in-law's senior, possesses more resources to break this damaging cold war. First of all, her older age brings with it more life experience. The mother-in-law has survived the relationship with <u>her</u> mother-in-law. She has, in addition, spent decades domesticating her own husband, turning him from a masculine hunk with limited awareness, communication skills and partnership conceptualization, into a manageable functioning partner. She has argued with phone repairmen, bank managers, annoying neighbors, sloppy painters, absentee gardeners, unavailable pediatricians, inflexible school tuition committees, door-to-door salesmen, abusive employees, cranky siblings and inept automobile repairmen. She has seen it all. She has become skilled at problem solving with individuals who annoy her to death.

Secondly, in terms of relationships, whether it be with "blood" or "water" relatives or friends, she has acquired the wisdom of avoiding the difficult people and concentrating on the enjoyable ones. And when it is a blood relative involved, whether it be a sibling, a child, or a parent, all of whom she correctly deems non-discardable, she has learned how to function civilly to allow life to proceed. She has learned what to say, when to say it, in front of whom <u>not</u> to say it, what works and what does not work. She has learned when to use a heavy hand and when to tiptoe. At her age, she has a well of survival skills.

Thirdly, her advanced age and experience have taught her what is truly important in life and what is nonsense. She knows intellectually that she always wants to stay close to her son. She wants to be very involved with his children who do, after all, carry on the family name. She therefore knows that she must eventually make peace with her daughter-in-law. The latter runs the house that she knows she must have a lifetime connection with. She is aware that it is just a question of time before she bites the bullet and accepts her daughter-in-law with her perceived impossible personality and alleged parenting deficiencies. She must accept the daughter-in-law's ideas and values which she deems witless. Hopefully, she will wisely select that sooner is better than later, because life is short, and health problems and other life setbacks hit everyone, so why not clean up the mess quickly.

Lastly, the daughter-in-law, regardless of her IQ and built in talents and skills, is still wet behind the ears emotionally. She is exhausted by juggling a new marriage, new babies, running a house, financial pressures, lack of sleep, holding a job, trying to make new friends and hold on to old ones, trying to be a responsible party in community affairs, working to keep peace with her blood relatives, and trying to do it all putting on a happy face. It is highly unlikely that she has the stored up emotional security in sufficient quantity to deal with all of this, much less a critical, annoying mother-in-law. It is easier for her to chuck the latter than to have one of the higher priorities fail. The extraordinary effort to make peace cannot come from her.

So, in summary, the mother-in-law steeped in anger, pride, disappointment, hopelessness, and loneliness in this private struggle of hers, gets the additional burden of initiating and pursuing the thaw with her daughter-in-law. While it initially feels like a hopeless, unrewarded, unjustified and uncomfortable project, she must and will do it. Everyone will benefit from her effort.

# The Prognosis is Good to Excellent

One would think that considering the opposing vantage points of the mother-in-law—daughter-in-law in their classic syndrome, there would be little hope for future improvement. Not so. After studying many case histories of formerly battling adversaries, one can see a silver lining to this famous storm cloud. This optimistic prognosis may be attributed to three factors: the natural flexibility of the human being, the maturing of the daughter-in-law, and the mellowing of the mother-in-law.

Note that the prognosis is not <u>all</u> excellent, unfortunately. Many factors can prevent repair in certain cases. If the young couple lives far away from <u>his</u> parents, the get-togethers are usually spread apart, and the early strife, if it has occurred, has fewer opportunities of being mended. Second, if irreversible harmful words or actions occur early in the relationship, before they are sidestepped or prevented, it can be a deathblow for future harmony. Third, if the conflict picks up family members on each side who support the strife for one reason or another rather than trying to soothe it, it will gain momentum rather than run its usually self-limiting course. Fourth, where either the mother-in-law or daughter-in-law is so limited emotionally due to her own personal baggage, then she cannot proceed forward, and would probably stay stuck in the wrong position. There are many other variations.

The incredible flexibility of men and women, especially women, is a powerful force to project a cheerful resolution of the mother-in-law—daughter-in-law dilemma. Peace, pure and simple, is easier on the system than war. Warmth is far more attractive than cold separation. Support of loved ones is much more cozy than detached loneliness. Like litters of puppies that crawl all over one another and tumble into each other and eventually fall asleep leaning against one another, people gravitate toward supportive closeness. Living life with its unpredictable vicissitudes surrounded by loving family members helps people to survive. So a strong vote here goes to the human tendency to smooth the rough spots of daily living.

The second large reason to be upbeat about the future of mothers-in-law and daughters-in-law, is the expected maturing of the daughter-in-law. Over a period of time, hopefully not too long, she will build up her self-confidence. She will be less self conscious, less worried about what people will think of her if she feels she is on the side of correctness. She will have a more appropriate sense of what is important in this world and less threatened by every little negative glitch that comes along. She will have an improved overview of proper family relations and which areas are worth fighting for.

She will gradually look at the mother-in-law as an aging matriarch who is not so bad after all. Her mother-in-law's opinions and attitudes will start being lumped into the typical pontifications of older people, like uncles, like grandparents, like her friend's parents. What her mother-in-law preaches begins to sound typical and predictable, and less threatening because they are not aimed at her in particular. She will see her kids excited about the mother-in-law's visits, and to her surprise, she will see her kids flock around her mother-in-law with genuine affection. She might allow herself to take a big step, asking her former adversary to babysit while she and her husband run off on an overnight rendezvous. In time, she will find herself moving a notch closer, asking her mother-in-law her opinion about something like wallpaper or a recipe or which pictures of a group to enlarge. If progress continues, she might even accidentally call her "Mom" before she realized what she was actually saying. She might greet her after a while with a hug or a light kiss. If she is an aware person, she might see a change in her mother-in-law in response to this emerging warmth. Her mother-in-law might become more complimentary about the good things she sees around the household and diminish the list of negative comments.

So the daughter-in-law's evolution into a seasoned matriarch of her own budding family will allow more appropriate attitudes and responses to her husband's mother. She will see the latter as a loving grandmother, a very essential factor in her kids' development. She will see her as a somewhere between an aunt and her true mother, which is really terrific when you think of it, especially if she has the aware participation of her husband, THE SON. Her husband does have the capacity of throwing the mother-in-law—daughter-in-law relationship in either direction. If he is wise and he is secure in his marriage and he sees the positive feeling his mother brings along with her on her visits, he will encourage his wife appropriately in the direction of even further closeness.

The third huge piece of the puzzle with a happy ending is the mellowing of the former combative mother-in-law. On an over-simplified basis, the mother-in-law can grow accustomed to many of her daughter-in-law's deficiencies as she would with any of life's annoyances, like tight shoes, like a dripping bathtub, like a cold sore, like an awful haircut. Realistically, though, she will start seeing her daughter-in-law as being not so bad, but rather just another overwhelmed new wife trying to cope and learn on the job and please everyone dependent on her. She will be reminded of her own initiation into the role of wife and young mother, with her own struggles and insecurities (and her own problems with <u>her</u> mother-in-law)! She will start feeling great love for the grandchildren despite the fact that they both look exactly like her daughter-in-law or one of <u>her</u> parents. With increasing visits, she will find her son's home increasingly comfortable and inviting. She will start seeing some of the talents of her son's wife that she never allowed herself heretofore to acknowledge. She might begin to see her son happier than she ever remembered despite the current pressure of running a family and making a living. She sees him relaxed, genuinely happy to come home, and giggling a lot more often than he did growing up. In all fairness, she will give the overdue credit to the love of his wife.

The mother-in-law will adjust and problem solve in the usual expert manner that her life experience has taught her. She will become less emotionally involved than she felt when her daughter-in-law first appeared on the scene. She will be distracted by the normal busy good times and bad times that life brings with it. She will have a more casual overview of this past irritating relationship. The lens of her focus will slide from closeup to panorama. Her other children and grandchildren, her siblings, her husband, all will come back to the forefront, and life will go on. Holiday celebrations, family dinners, school plays, trips to the dentist and grocery shopping will return to the daily check list.

The prognosis <u>is</u> good to excellent.

# Interview #1—Mother-in-Law

What were your expectations?

*To have 3 daughters, all getting along, and a close family.*

What is actually happening or what did happen?

*Daughter-in-law #1 started out all loving to excess until there was one disagreement. She then proceeded to "divide and conquer". In actuality, she divided my son to conquer him, and try to turn him against me. I did not agree with her "sense of entitlement" which she, as a narcissistic person, could not tolerate. We distanced. I continue to visit and see the children where mostly I am treated as a "non-person." She responds only to questions, never showing interest in me. She talks very rudely in a fresh manner. She is very child-centered, which is the same as self-centered.*

*Daughter-in-law #2 started out cool and aloof, but was able to rebound without any disagreement. She turned out to be loving, kind, considerate and giving. She knows how to express interest. A good*

151

relationship ensues, and we continue to keep in touch and visit, including overnight holidays.

*My third son is not yet married.*

What steps have you taken to change things—from within or without?

*The steps taken with daughter-in-law #1 are to keep visiting the children and avoid confrontations (unless absolutely necessary!), and to show the children that I am a presence in their lives. I confronted daughter-in-law #1 about the fact that her children never see us interact. She absorbed this because she is child-centered, and now talks to me in front of the children. I accepted the fact that she might be unhappy not to personalize too much. She is rude and fresh to other people including her husband, my son. I have tried to tolerate from within that I can't get everyone to love me as I am, and I cannot love everyone as they are.*

What can you do to make yourself feel better?

*To feel better, I try to engage in a situation that I enjoy, and to be with people who satisfy my emotional needs and make me feel good. These are generally soft spoken, easy people. I shy away from strong, domineering types.*

What is your prognosis or outlook for the future?

*My prognosis is to try not to allow any severances of relationship with daughter-in-law #1. I hope that one day, she will pull out of herself to see me as a fallible person who is older, and therefore show respect.*

## Interview #2—Daughter-in-Law

What were your expectations for your relationship with your mother-in-law before you got married?

*I expected my mother-in-law to be to be just like my mother. I expected her to understand me completely as if she had raised me from infancy—obviously unfair expectations. I had heard horrible mother-in-law stories but I never thought that my mother-in-law could ever be wrong and not understand me. Those were my expectations.*

Is it that you liked her so much initially when you met her that you just assumed that you would get along?

*When I first met her, she was a little taken aback, because my husband and I had been dating for all of one month, and this was the first time he brought a girl home. I didn't know that, of course. He didn't tell me. So, she indeed was a little taken aback. I can't say she was staring me up and down but I can't say she was completely relaxed either. And after three months, we got engaged, so to say the least she had a reason to be scared. However, from my point of view, I knew that I loved her son. I knew that he loved me. What was her problem? Initially, I think she was trying to make herself likeable because she didn't know what else to do. She didn't know me and I just assumed that she would like me and that everything would be fine.*

Does she have a good relationship with your husband?

*My husband is the baby by 7 years and the oldest is 12 years older than he. I would say that she very much babies him. She doesn't always respect him as an adult, and quite often, she tells him what she thinks he should do. They don't have a terrible relationship, but they certainly don't have a very good one.*

So what's the reality of your relationship with her now?

*Now, ten years later, it's much better than it was the first six years.*

What was it like the first six years?

*The first 2 ½ years were complicated because I was young. I was very opinionated. I thought I knew everything. I'm very strong willed and my mother-in-law is exactly the same. So, we clashed a lot. She is very strong willed. She has her opinion about everything including what color one should or shouldn't like. If she gave me a gift, and I didn't jump up and down and say I absolutely adored it, she would take it personally. If she liked a dress for me but I didn't like it, she would try to give me the reasons why I should like it. So that's how it was difficult over the first 2 ½ years. After that, we moved into our first home and things became a little bit better. Then my father-in-law became very ill. He was diagnosed with cancer. As things got worse, I had to bite my tongue more and more, so we didn't necessarily run into these big, drawn out fights. I did, though, feel very much resentment and anger and I couldn't let it out because she was living a nightmare. So I'd say that during those 4 ½ years of my father-in-law's illness, I had a lot of stuff that was kept bottled up.*

Every day stuff or stuff involving you and the kids?

*Everything! Everyday stuff, stuff involving the kids, my husband, our vacations, what we were going to do in the house, what we weren't going to do in the house. Everything, everything. She had a lot to say about everything.*

Were you asking her or she offered it?

*Oh, no! I never needed to ask. It was always unsolicited, very much so. On the other hand, she was a very loving person, very caring, very giving, and really emotionally very giving. During that time that my father-in-law was ill, she was rarely around for the kids in person. She wasn't babysitting and wasn't taking them out to do things, and that's because at any moment, her husband could die. So she wasn't living a life at all. And I didn't know how much of that was because of her circumstance with his illness or because that's really the way she was. Her other grandchildren lived so far away that I didn't have anything to judge it by. What was she like before he was ill? And so my assumption, unfortunately, was that she isn't such a wonderful grandmother because she just isn't. I didn't realize how much of it was because she was taking care of my father-in-law. I found out after he died that she is really quite a wonderful grandmother, very available, very accessible, and very much willing to be around. She comes to us for the Sabbath quite often because it is easier for her to come to us than for us to come to her. I really admire how she has gone on with her life after not having one for close to five years. I think a lot of it was my perspective, kind of a wrong perspective, of the way things were.*

Were any steps taken to improve the relationship?

*We had one huge fight within a year after my father in law died. I'm not sure what exactly it was. My husband and I were going to do something with the kids, but then our plans changed. We had mentioned to her what we were going to be doing, but we never told her that our plans had changed, and we were going to the Bronx Zoo or something like that instead. And there really was no reason to tell her anything altogether. It was just something we happened to mention and why we couldn't be with her that Sunday. She was very needy, especially the first year my father-in-law died. If we came for a Sabbath stay, she would press. "Why don't we stay through Sunday?" That kind of thing. Or why were we leaving so early Sunday morning and not staying through Sunday afternoon? It was never enough. So we happened to mention that we had plans, changed our plans, and didn't inform her. She called her son the following day at work and said to him, "How come you lied to me?" She was very, very angry, and confronted him and told him that we lied to her. This was while he was working. She actually interfered with his work to yell at him. That goes back to the whole thing where I don't think she respects him as an adult. He called me, mortified, and told me, and I said, "Are you going to put a stop to it?" And he said, "There is no stopping her. This is the way she is." I said, "No one has ever called me a liar before and no one is about to." So I literally got in my car and drove to her house. When she opened the door, I just started screaming. I think I just lost my mind after holding stuff back for so long. This was too hurtful, and despite many of the attempts to bite my lip and be understanding of her, I felt like she didn't understand us at all. So for about 45 minutes, I really ripped into her. I was really cruel and I said some things that were really horrible. She screamed back, too, and she said some pretty terrible things as well and was being very defensive, of course. And when it was all over, about a week later, she called me and she apologized. Despite the fact that I said some pretty terrible things, she was very apologetic. I just thought that was a really big deal, considering she is such a control freak and she is so manipulative in general and very opinionated. For her to sit back and say, "Well, maybe some of this is right and I'm sorry." was huge. Since then, we have had a much better relationship. It really cleared the air. Not that there haven't been bumps in the road in the meantime, but it really cleared the air.*

What do you see in the future?

*I see the relationship only improving, I think, because she is understanding us a little bit more and I'm understanding her a lot more. I don't think there is going to be much give on her part. I think there is going to have to be more on our part, and I think that we are both willing to do it. I think it has to be me and my husband, not just one or the other.*

Why more from you than her?

*I would think that for a mother-in-law, it's gotta be hard. I look at my boys and I think that when they grow up, they need to get married to their wives, and their wives need to be their priority. For whatever reason, life just works better for a couple when the husband puts his wife first and the wife has to put her husband first. But for whatever reason, I think that a woman could still manage a good relationship with her mother-in-law without it being mutually exclusive. I think that for a son, a mother has really got to take a back seat. She is not in the picture to the same extent, and as hard as that is to swallow, I think it is a reality.*

*I have two very different sons. One is very outgoing and assertive, and one is very timid and shy and quiet. With the assertive one, I'm probably going to have a decent relationship with that daughter-in-law. He's probably going to marry somebody who is a little bit his opposite. But with my shy kid, I can just see there being tension, real tension. I may be all wrong, but I don't think I'm that wrong. I'm starting to see it from my mother-in-law's point of view even though I haven't experienced it at all. Her son is the quiet, shy, meeker kind of good boy, and he definitely married a very strong willed, opinionated woman, and I feel for her. So I think it has to be more give on my part. I'm the one in the relationship with her son. She is all alone. That's the other part of it. She's all alone and she's not an old woman by any means. To be all alone when you are that vivacious and you have known your husband since you were 14, and she is now 69, it's just so hard. So I think there is more compassion on my end, and with that, there is more responsibility on my end to be better. The other reason I feel kind of the responsibility for it to be better is because she has a daughter who is in Israel, and she has a daughter who is in Arizona. Those are her only two daughters. She has a son who doesn't like planes and the relationship just isn't there. She has another son who is 45 and still single, and so, I feel like we're it. The daughter who is in Israel is too far away. And the daughter who is in Arizona is divorced. It's just a very complicated situation. I'm not tooting my horn, but I'm just saying that all the family enjoyment she's getting is from our end.*

# Interview #3—Mother-in-Law

*In writing this, I have to look back on my life, my values and how I reared my children. My sons were raised to be independent adults and so they also chose strong- willed partners, who knew what they wanted and didn't settle for anything less.*

*I had always hoped for a close knit family, children, grandchildren living within a 30 mile radius to me, close with each other, with cousins, aunts, uncles, etc. Well, I got half of my wish. God works in mysterious ways. Both my sons and their families live in Israel less than 30 miles from each other, and they have a good relationship with each other.*

*When my son called me from Israel to tell me he was engaged to a wonderful girl, a Sabra, I felt joy and empty at the same time. I could not share in the usual rituals of engagement, or wedding plans. I met her on her wedding day in a hotel lobby, one hour prior to the ceremony. We were both nervous but there was an instant rapport, a* *warm chemistry between us. I was the wonderful mother of her husband-to-be. She was the <u>daughter</u> I never had. Her warmth and her loving, giving personality created the beginning of a relationship that grew better and better each year. Unfortunately, her mother died in an auto accident, and I became her "mother". We look forward to seeing each other when I make my yearly trip to Israel. This summer, we planned a vacation together, spent much more time with each other, and had a wonderful time. At this point in my life, this is the best I can hope for until I retire, and then maybe take more than one a trip a year to Israel.*

*My other son married a lovely girl, an American. She is quite different. She has parents who visit two and three times a year. She has cousins who live in the same neighborhood in Israel. She has siblings and quite an extended family. She is very close to her family. Our personalities are very different and I feel I am truly a "mother-in-law". She does not need a very close relationship with me. I don't feel that there is anything I can do to bring us closer, but it is okay. That's the way it is. I accept it, and do the best I can in not comparing these two women. I love them both, but in very different ways. I have one daughter and one daughter-in-law.*

*Prognosis: Who knows what the future holds?*

## Interview #4—Daughter-in-Law

*I got married when I graduated college and I honestly don't remember having any expectations from my mother-in-law. My situation was actually a unique one because my family lives outside of New York and my in-laws are from New York. From the time I met my in-laws, they have always taken me in with much warmth and treated me like a daughter. My mother-in-law took really good care of me before we got married, and always went out of her way for me in various scenarios. In this regard, I suppose that my expectations were for everything to remain the same.*

*When we got married, I was in school and my husband was working. Then we switched roles for the next two years. My mother-in-law was very supportive of me. When I had my kids, she either took care of me in her house or she came to my house. Every year, she babysits for my kids so that my husband and I can go away. In this respect, she met my expectations in our early years. She is now* in her mid-fifties and works very hard. She is physically not there for me as much as in the past. We don't go to her house anymore for the weekends because having us all is a little stressful for her. She prefers to come to our house. She will always come through for me when I need her, but she needs me more than she had in the past. For example, I usually cook a lot for her when she has a family party.

On a more emotional level, she is very accepting of who I am, yet I know she can't fully relate to everything I do. This comes out at times in indirect ways, and they annoy me, but I ultimately understand her because we are truly different people in many ways. For example, I spend more money on things than she would and she probably thinks that I have very little concept of money. She will make comments on how I should buy my meat in Brooklyn and freeze it in bulk. She also can't really relate to my wanting to stay at home with my kids rather than work. She tries to mask her comments but I know she feels that my education was a waste, and every day that I don't work, I become a less marketable professional.

The steps that I take to improve the "bumps" in our relationship are to fully communicate who I am to her and to also always understand her perspective when she makes comments as mentioned above. Having this perspective in mind keeps those comments at the level of being "annoying" versus anything more involved than that.

The prognosis is very good as long as I continue to communicate with her.

# Interview #5—Mother-in-Law

What were your expectations?

*I expected to have a close, friendly relationship with my daughters-in-law. Having three sons, there would be no comparisons made to a daughter, and I believed that would enhance the relationship. I hoped to talk to them often, and as a woman, share some of my life experiences as a "wise elder", to be a sounding board as I had been with my sons throughout their lives. I expected to see them on a regular basis. My husband and I visited with our parents regularly with our children. It was understood that significant events would be shared by extended family.*

What actually transpired?

*Boy, was I in for a surprise! I think of myself as generally a very accepting, non-judgmental person. I try not to be confrontational, as I am not very comfortable with it.*

*At this point, let me say that I believe there are lessons to be learned in life and that situations present themselves for such a purpose. Wow! I have a lot to learn. I have three completely different daughters-in-law coming from very different backgrounds and geographical locations, with different emotional and psychological needs. They married at a later age than I, worked or are working while raising their children, and have very strong ideas. They expect to make decisions without input from parents or in-laws. They read all the current books on whatever topic they are dealing with at the moment, and believe this gives them the expertise necessary to make sound decisions, with experience not relevant to the matter.*

*They seem to believe that it is their husbands' responsibility to maintain the relationship with me. I find that most of the interaction between us is done through my sons to me, especially if it is a request for something, such as babysitting arrangements, etc.*

*One of the most painful truths that I had to acknowledge and learn to accept was the change in the relationship between my sons and myself. It is the loss of a bond, a closeness that has been transferred to their wives. It is healthy and necessary, but still a loss that I learned I had to mourn in order to move on. I had to acknowledge that the only thing that I could change was myself and my reactions to a given situation. I have been a mother-in-law for eight years. It has been frustrating and hurtful at times, but I have had to examine and re-examine my participation in these very important relationships. I have gone for counseling to help me* understand my feelings and examine my expectations. I feel obsolete much of the time.

What steps are being taken, if any, by the parties involved for improvement?

*I have learned that if I can change my behavior, leave room for others to respond, more often than not, I am OK with the outcome. A major change that I found helpful was to keep lowering my expectations, resulting in less disappointment and unhappiness. I often say that I feel that mothering is the only occupation in which the longer you do it, the less you know. Humor can be helpful!*

*I am working on learning to state my needs and desires clearly and directly, without assuming they should know them automatically, and without any blame or guilt inferred. I have backed off from my children, and find that if given enough space, they reach out to me. Calls and visits are less often than I would like, and I am learning to be OK with that. Again, I have found that lower expectations results in happier feelings.*

*I recently heard that a thought is like a seed that grows. We have the power to nourish it in a constructive or destructive manner. Every day, I conscientiously nurture positive thoughts and release negative ones, especially concerning my children and the families. There are times that I resent having to work so hard at these relationships, but this is the reality that I live with, and these relationships are among the most important ones to me.*

What's your projection/prognosis for the future?

*I have experienced positive changes with my daughters-in-law and myself. One daughter-in-law has many of her own issues that need to be addressed, and until that is done, the relationship is problematic, and only time will tell. I feel optimistic that these relationships will continue to improve. As mothers, it has always been our role to guide and nurture our children, but the rules change on us as they become adults. Our children teach us to be flexible. I am so flexible I fear I'm going to one day snap from all the bending that I am doing! I also hear "bite your tongue". I worry there will be no tongue left to bite.*

*After all the years of hearing mother-in-law jokes. I realize that I am not unique in my feelings, that they have been experienced by mothers forever. I now have a better understanding of the actions that result in these jokes. "In-lawing" is a very complex relationship. (My observation is that fathers don't seem to have the same reactions to as many issues as mothers have.)*

*I hope and pray to be around to watch my daughters-in-law become mothers-in-law. JUSTICE, JUSTICE!*

## Interview #6 - Daughter-in-Law

What were your expectations of a mother-in-law—daughter-in-law relationship?

*I was looking forward to this relationship. First, because I love relationships and I love talking to people and love establishing relationships. I was definitely looking forward to it, and I thought "Why wouldn't someone be so happy that I was marrying her son?" I would enjoy that, and we would go from there and it would be a mutually happy relationship". And I have a good relationship with my own mother, but I thought it would be cool to have another good relationship with a woman. I love relationships with women and I love knowing that it could happen, especially with whoever my husband's mother was going to be. I thought we'd have a great friendly kind of relationship. I thought whoever his mother might be, it would be equal and the same. I was definitely looking forward to it, and eager for it to be good.*

How are things going? What is the real scenario?

*My mother in law, it's not her fault, is very limited emotionally. She is definitely limited intellectually and she is limited socially.*

Which you didn't know about before…

*When I first me her it was obvious, but I thought I could change her. But there is just no way. She is older, in her late 70s, and it's difficult dealing with a limited person. I would say we have almost no relationship. She tries harder than I do, which is my fault. I could try a little bit harder. She will call me once a week just to say "hi". It is very formal, and it's not very caring.*

Do you think it has to do with her age?

*I think it has to do with her age. I also think she is limited. She is really…she is not slow, but there is something slow about her. She just doesn't…she's a very nice person and she's kind. She's very kind. I think anyone who meets her thinks she is nice, but she has no friends. She has never really had friends. She has very little relationship with her other grandchildren or her other children. It's all very limited. My husband is such an emotional, open, and warm human being—everything the opposite of her. That's why I think it was so shocking to me that a mother and son could be so different. To me, that was really shocking.*

How are you going to go about changing it?

*I have totally given up.*

After how long?

*We are married 5 years after we dated 3 years. So the first year of dating, I didn't even think about it. I didn't discuss it with my husband. I thought, "It will get better", or "I'll make it better". Then it was the cause of tension in our marriage for a few years because to me also, the grandparent/grandchild relationship was very, very important. Seeing how my parents were with my children, I just didn't see how there was any other way. You know, they are so warm. My parents are like second parents to my children, so I felt that there was no question that just as they needed to be like that, my mother-in-law especially needed to be like that. When it didn't happen, I would take it out a lot on my husband because he wasn't helping to change it. He would try to explain to me "I can't change it, this is the way she is, there is nothing I could do". That was it. It is still, sometimes, a source of contention because I don't want to spend as much time with them. But, he feels more guilt, so that he wants his children to see them. My father-in-law recently passed away, and now, especially because his father died, I think he wants the kids to see her more; but I think, on the other hand, he knows how uncomfortable this is. My kids don't really know who she is. If she comes to the house, they often will say, sometimes even in front of her, "Who is this lady"? It's very sad. She sends checks in the mail for their birthdays. That's it. Nothing personal, nothing emotional. It's sad. I think it's sad for her. I'm not as sad about it as I was in the beginning because there is nothing I can do. It's a shame. She is older, this is the way her life is. She has no intention of changing. It is sad because she could have had a warm relationship with her grandchildren.*

How is her relationship with your husband?

*Good. Nothing would ever come up negative from him about her because he is very respectful to the point that I could learn from him—very, very respectful. Part of the respect is due to guilt. If he is not good to her, that bothers him. He doesn't think about closeness with her. We're his family now. I am not worried at all that he is going to be like his father or that he's going to be like his mother, or that he thinks that their behavior is normal. In the beginning, I used to think he must think this is normal because this is what he grew up with, but he doesn't. He just knows that there is nothing one could do. The relationship is fine. He doesn't think about it much, and she probably doesn't think about it either.*

So your prognosis?

*Recently, since my father in law died, I feel a little more guilty that I don't...that there's nothing more I could do emotionally with her. We don't talk about anything more than "How's the weather, how's the kids, what's your day like?" But I think I could probably do more calling, or just make more of an effort to see her. She doesn't drive so she doesn't come out here. We are only together if we go there or we pick her up. I wouldn't say I've made more of an effort, but I think about it more, so maybe I could try and do that. Also, what's sad to me is the fact that my husband's first wife passed away, and here I was marrying him pretty soon after his wife died. His parents, especially his mother, never, ever greeted me warmly or said anything to me like "We're so happy you came into his life. We're so happy that he found happiness." Nothing along those lines and nothing to even say that "Now, he has a life and family and that's great." Nothing. I just thought this was very sad also.*

# Interview #7—Mother-in-Law

How are you doing with your newest daughter-in-law?

*My daughter-in-law is a good person and very well meaning. She is very bright and has a professional degree.*

*Her work and social life are her highest priorities. She is just not a housewife type. My problem is that I see that things are not running well. She is not gifted with ease and efficiency managing house and career. The house is a mess and the sweet children that she chose to bring into this world are sadly neglected. It hurts to admit that I have trouble visiting my own son's home.*

*I only wish that somewhere in a girl's upbringing, whether it be in her own family or from courses in school, that she be taught what is most important. Care for husband, children and home have to come first, before friends and job.*

*Don't get me wrong. Socializing and satisfaction at work are very much fulfilling. But...if you have babies and still want to have it all, you'd better be highly organized, or something is going to suffer. If a new mother like her is not blessed with such efficiency, she really ought to consider a nanny or full-time help. Or, maybe she should just defer her career until the kids are older.*

*Meanwhile, my heart goes out to my son and precious grandchildren. I wish it were different.*

## Interview #8—Daughter-in-Law

What were your expectations for your relationship with your mother-in-law before you got married?

*I don't remember really having any expectations. I just assumed it would be the same way that my mother and grandmother are with each other, the role model I had for mother—mother-in-law relationship which was always a good relationship. I just assumed it would be the same. I didn't really have any specific expectations.*

And they have a very good relationship?

*Very good.*

What is the reality?

*The reality is that it is very similar to my mother's relationship with her mother-in-law. There is a lot of mutual respect and a lot of family closeness. I don't really talk to her on a daily basis at all, but whenever I call, I'm very comfortable talking to her and I respect her opinion. She doesn't call here on a daily basis either, but whenever she does call the kids are excited to talk to here and I'm happy to catch up on things.*

Is she close with your husband?

*They were very, very close when he was growing up and they are still at that same level of closeness, meaning they love each other and they respect each other. I wouldn't know if you would call it an adult close relationship. They don't talk about deep things now, but they talk with fondness about funny things that used to happen on vacations. I don't know if he would call his mother for advice about something but he would definitely let her know funny things that the kids said. They enjoy each other's company, but they don't rely on each other for moral support.*

Do you do anything to make it a closer relationship?

*I make an effort to make sure that my kids are close with their grandparents, making sure the kids get on the phone to wish them a Good Shabbos (Sabbath). I make sure that if we haven't seen them in a week or two, that we go out there on a Sunday afternoon to see them. But I don't really make efforts on a personal level to have a personal friendship with my mother-in-law. Maybe once in a while I'll tell her something just because I feel like it will make her feel good to know that I wanted to talk to her about such and such a thing. This is not because I really need to talk to her but more because I think that it would bring closeness.*

You feel like you have friends and family in your life that you depend on, and you don't depend on her?

*Not in a bad way. If she would happen to be here at a time when I was going through something, I would love to talk to her about it. If she happens not to be here, then she's not the first person that I think of that "I'd better call her and talk about it".*

Issues with your children—do they involve her at all?

*Do you mean decisions?*

Yes.

*We had a major type of decision last year that we were deciding working on. We have a child whose birthday is two days away from the official class cutoff date. He makes the cutoff technically, but I was thinking that maybe he would have the advantage if he stayed back a year. He would be the oldest in the class, instead of going ahead and being the youngest in the class. I thought about that for six months. I definitely mentioned it to her. She is a kindergarten teacher so she was the perfect one to talk to about it, but her personality is very much restrained. She is not a meddler. So her answer is always like "I know you'll make the right decision, and either way, it will be fine and he's great". You know, he's her grandson. She is not very opinionated or pushy which on one hand makes it easier to talk to her, but on the other hand, it also makes it kind of useless to talk to her because she doesn't really say anything.*

What's your prognosis for the future—just continuing the same way it is now?

*Yes, very much. She retired this year, so I already see the next stage in her life but not in a hypothetical way. I see what it actually is. She goes to classes and she has friends and she goes dancing. She just doesn't rely on her family for her social interactions, so it makes it easier for me not to always feel obligated to be her social outlet, because she has her own set of friends. We enjoy family when we are together, but I don't feel pressured that I have to entertain my in-laws all the time, because I know they are very busy.*

## Interview #9—Mother-in-Law


*When you were growing up and you hear stories about the constant battles that mothers-in-law and daughters-in-law have, your first reaction is that mine will be different. I will do everything in my power to make it work.*

*When your son is dating your future daughter-in-law, you are starting to feel so close like you are really bonding. It's quite a letdown when the relationship is not what you anticipated. Due to the fact that my son was so engrossed in his studies, my relationship with my future daughter-in-law was initially very close. In fact, I never would think of her as an in-law, but like a daughter. So my expectations were quite high going into this relationship.*

*My hopes were deflated when I made the error of assuming that my perception of what should work for their family, with suggestions made by me, were not taken very well. My input was taken as a constant criticism, rather than what I thought could only be helpful due to years of more life experiences. Rule number one is to never put your son in the middle. It only creates more dissention. When you see your son agreeing with his wife, it hurts, but you know that's the way is should be. It's better that way. It's their life. I know now how important it is to choose words very carefully. Most things that I have said, which I thought were most harmless, have been misconstrued and have created too much pain. So now, being older and more experienced, I try to be a good listener. I try to be agreeable even though it goes against my better judgment, because I really feel my input could be of use if they did it my way.*

*My most important issue are the grandchildren, the children of my daughter-in-law and son. I would never want anything to jeopardize that relationship. I can look way from any negatives as long as it will safeguard the relationship that is so dear to me. Any adversities with the mother are not worth jeopardizing the relationship with the grandchildren.*

*I am a firm believer in airing out any negative feelings and getting past it. However, when you are dealing with an individual who is very sensitive to your suggestions and opinions, then my behavior has to change and I have to be the one to make it work. There is too much at stake mere. My belief is that as long as I keep the relationship healthy and strong with my grandchildren, the rest will take care of itself.*

## Interview #10—Daughter-in-Law


What were your expectations for the relationship before you got married?

*I don't know I if I really had any expectations. I was probably more nervous. I got married at the age of 22. It was just more of a fear, you know. You always hear about the mother-in-law story. I was just hoping that we would get along. I was hoping that I would live up to her expectations. I was marrying her youngest son, taking her baby away from her and I just hoped that she wasn't going to resent that. I just really looked forward to having a good relationship, not as good as with my mother because she's not my mother, but having another friend in my circle.*

What was the reality of your relationship once you got married?

*I've been truly blessed, because the reality was much more strange. I love my mother dearly, but over the course of the years, my mother-in-law is just, I think, the most perfect mother-in-law in the world. Quite honestly, I feel closer, not to take anything away from my mother, but I'm absolutely closer to my mother-in-law than I am with my mom. She has been totally supportive. She is a friend. I truly feel that she considers me as close as a daughter to her as her son is to her as a son. I'm probably closer to her than her own daughter.*

Why is that?

*Part of that is the distance factor because her own daughter is out of the country. Part of it is just a click of a personality. This is going to sound corny, but I think she absolutely cherishes the relationship that I have with my husband. She doesn't have her husband any more and she just sees how happy we are. I think that as a mother, if your child is happy, the person that is making your child happy must go up several notches. She has been the opposite of the absentee grandmother. Even before we had kids, she made it a point, when my husband was in medical school, if not every Sunday, then every other Sunday, she would take us out to dinner. When the kids were young, she was at our house every Sunday. And she calls now, knowing that her son is not home during the day. She will call me at 3:00 P.M. to talk to me and then she will call again in the evening to talk to him. So it is independent. I truly feel that she is not calling me as her son's wife, but we have come to a point where she is calling me as her "daughter". She is really a super lady. I feel bad because I can't imagine most of my friends having the relationship that I do.*

185

What's going to improve to make this relationship an even better one?

*It's hard to say. There's never really been anything bad about the relationship. The funny thing is that she definitely does have her own opinions. Whenever she expresses her opinion, she starts off with, "OK, tell me to mind my own business, but..." She totally respects whether we take it or not. She is giving us her advice just for what it is, with no expectations on her part for us to listen to her. "You are your own people and you have to do what you have to do, but I'm a 70 plus year old woman so I need to share with you what I feel about a certain situation". There has been nothing to improve. I really can't think of anything.*

And the prognosis?

*The prognosis is for a wonderful relationship. I would hope that she is with us for many, many, many more years, so we can continue the relationship that we have right now. This is the strangest thing, but when we had built our house, we happened to have added a separate kitchen and a spare bedroom downstairs. I kid with her all the time, and you are not going to find many people that say this, but her rent keeps going up and whatever, and I say to her to feel free to move in with us. I mean this with a full heart. I don't mean that I would want her in my living quarters, but, because of the separate little area, she could come and go as she pleases. I said to her, "If you ever want to give up your apartment, you know you have your own little kitchen downstairs." I don't think she would ever take me up on that because, as much as she loves us, she is very independent and she relishes her privacy. When she comes to join us for a weekend, and I try to have her over as much as possible, she just can't wait to leave—not because she doesn't love spending time with us, but I guess when you get to a certain age, your bed is your bed. She loves her solitude. She balances it by coming, but then being very happy to leave at the same time. I know she would never take me up on my offer, but I am very sincere when I offer it. I would never tell this to my mother because I don't want her to be hurt, but they are just two different kinds of people.*

*When I go Mother's Day card shopping for my mother-in-law, I can't find one that's gushy enough. I'll look for the really mushy, "How much you've done for us...", because she has been really supportive in being there physically and monetarily. I'm at a point where I don't need the $100 check, but she insists every so often, "Put this in the savings account." For Succoth holiday, when we buy the "lulav" and "esrog", she does this. This is her love, her giving to her children. So when it is Mother's Day, I'll just stand there and take a long time to look for the card that just has the perfect wording. The opposite is with my mother, not in a bad way, but I'll look for your standard "Hi I love you. Have a happy day. Wish you all the best." My requirements for my mother-in-law are much, much more explicit than for my mom.*

## Interview #11—Mother-in-Law

*We had mixed emotions when our son came home from his trip to Japan and told us that he was madly in love with a Japanese girl.*

*Being that he was at the time in his thirties and still unmarried, we were happy for him. But we did not know anything about the young girl, and did know how we would react.*

*We took an instant liking to her when we met her. She is quiet and delicate, and above all, she makes our son very happy.*

*They are married over two years now and they seem to complement each other very well.*

*Our relationship with them is open, honest and friendly. We always enjoy their company. They are content with their life as is, and so far there is no talk or a hint about starting a family. We realize that it is their decision to make, but we feel that it is a big void in our lives not having grandchildren. Otherwise, we are very satisfied with our daughter-in-law. As a matter of fact, she is our very dear daughter.*

*Dr. Joseph Morris*

[Ruth to her mother-in-law, Naomi]

"...wherever you go, I will go; wherever you lodge, I will lodge; your people are my people, and your God is my God; where you die, I will die, and there I will be buried."

The Book of Ruth

Printed in the United States
45024LVS00005B/224